WORSHIP THE LORD!

Prayers for the Sunday Service

Louis Pratt

WORSHIP THE LORD!

Copyright © 1983 by
The C.S.S. Publishing Company, Inc.
Lima, Ohio

All rights reserved. No portion of this book may be reproduced or utilized in any form or by any means, electronic or mechanical including photocopying, without permission in writing from the publisher. Inquiries should be addressed to: The C.S.S. Publishing Company, Inc., 628 South Main Street, Lima, Ohio 45804.

Permission is given to reproduce this material as needed for congregational participation.

2332/ISBN 0-89536-580-4   PRINTED IN U.S.A.

TABLE OF CONTENTS

Calls to Worship.. 1

Prayers of Confession 11

General Prayers... 49

Poetry 71

Calls to Worship

1.

L. God is present to us,
P. *When we are present to one another.*
L. We, though many, are one body in Christ, and individually members of one another.
P. *Let us not think more highly of ourselves than we ought to think, since all persons are important members of the body of Christ.*

2.

L. The kingdom of God is yours today!
P. *Where do we have to go to enter it?*
L. You don't have to go anywhere — it is within you — just be aware!
P. *What must we do to enter?*
L. You don't have to do anything — just let go and let God take precedence in your lives. Cease pretending and start living as Christ has shown us.
P. *We open our lives to God and to one another so that we may truly live.*

3.

L. Listen! Your life is good. Whatever may have been, now is a new day in Christ.

P. In Christ we can receive our past, celebrate our present, and propose what our future shall be.
L. He has come to free us from the prison of self and make us whole and therefore holy.
P. Open the door to your heart, everyone, and let the light of life come in!

4.

L. God has accepted our past.
P. Help us accept our past, O Lord, both our participation in a renewing community and our responsibility for maintaining harmful traditions.
L. God has accepted our present.
P. Help us accept our present, Lord, and to affirm life regardless of our circumstances.
L. God holds out to us our future.
P. Help us to forget what is past, Lord, and to press on to the future that you desire for us.

5.

L. Why are you here?
P. To worship God with our prayers, our presence and our offerings.
L. With what should we present ourselves to God?
P. With joyful hearts and committed lives!

6.

L. Praise God for the freedom that is ours.
P. We are freed to reach out to one another.
L. Praise God for the future that is ours.
P. We are free from the past, free to help create our future.

7.

L. What does the Lord require of us?
P. To love justice, and to walk in peace.
L. With what shall we come before God?
P. With hearts tuned to his will and tongues bridled by truth.

8.

L. The Lord our God has set us free.
P. He is the source of our strength: we will trust in him.
L. Even darkness is not dark for God, and the night is as bright as the day for him.
P. In the darkest of our days we will continue to trust in the Lord and to walk in his ways.

9.

L. The Lord God has called us to be his disciples.
P. *We have heard your call, O God, and we will give you our best.*
L. The Lord God has called us to a state of belief in, and trust of, both him and our neighbor.
P. *We believe, O Lord; help us deal with our unbelief!*

10.

L. The Spirit of the Lord is upon us.
P. *He has anointed us as his agents to rout the forces of evil in this world and to establish his righteousness.*
L. And what does the Lord require of us?
P. *To do justice, to love mercy and kindness, and in all humility to see ourselves as we really are.*

11.

L. The glory of the Lord is upon us.
P. *He is our help and our salvation, always ready to help us when we are in trouble.*
L. Let us live as the holy people we are in Christ.
P. *With God as our helper, we will dare to live as he has called us to live.*

12.

L. God, the God of the Universe, calls us.
P. *Let us respond with our whole being, holding back nothing in our lives.*
L. Today is the day for God to work his salvation in our lives.
P. *We give ourselves to him and gladly take up our cross to follow him.*

13.

L. Trust in God!
P. *He is our Lord and our Redeemer — in his presence we renew our strength.*
L. Serve the Lord, for he expects great things of us.
P. *Our lives belong to him, and only in serving him do we find strength for living and rest for our souls.*

14.

L. Let us praise the Lord our God. He offers abundant life to all who follow him.
P. *We thank you, God, for our lives. Help us to live fully and completely.*

L. The Lord our God is a holy God, and he demands of us that we be like him.
P. *We will live our lives for God. All that keeps us from serving him, we will lay aside.*

15.
L. Seek God where he may be found.
P. *Let us seek him in the silence of the Sanctuary.*
L. He is ever present to those who seek him with discernment.
P. *He is as near as our neighbor, not as far as a star.*

16.
L. Return to the Lord, for he is quick to forgive.
P. *Forgive us, God, for lives that fall short of the forgiving love that Christ commanded us to live.*
L. As Christ has loved us, let us love one another.
P. *May God's Spirit inform our lives; may his wisdom guide us; and may his love enrich us.*

17.
L. Come, be yourself, and be joyful, for God has given us life!
P. *We come, joyful for life, but sometimes saddened because we do not live that life as fully as we should.*
L. Then come, hear the promise of Christ, be forgiven, and greater life shall be yours.
P. *We come without hesitation to praise God, the one who gives, forgives, and loves.*

18.
L. Praise the Lord, for his love enfolds us.
P. *He is ever near us, and quick to answer when we call.*
L. Take his yoke upon you, and all your burdens will seem lighter.
P. *Service to God renders all of life open and meaningful.*

19.
L. Let us thank the Lord for his steadfast love, for his wonderful works!
P. *The Lord is good, and his compassion is over all that he has made.*
L. Blessed be the Lord our God, who does wondrous things.
P. *Blessed be his glorious name forever; may his glory fill the whole earth.*

20.
- L. God sends us visions to keep us alert.
- P. Open our eyes, O God, that we may see.
- L. God speaks in many voices, through many people.
- P. Open our ears, O God, that we may hear.
- L. God gives us a part to play in the creation of his kingdom.
- P. Make us instruments of your love, O Lord.

21.
- L. Lift your heads and hold yourselves erect, for you are children of the living God!
- P. He has created us in his image; he enables us to grow spiritually and to meet the challenges of our day.
- L. God is a god of light, not darkness; he calls us to live as children of light, without fear of darkness.
- P. We will live our lives as ones confronted by the living God, as ones with little time for pettiness.

22.
- L. God is our Savior.
- P. He is ever in our midst.
- L. Those who come to him, who worship him in spirit and in truth, he will by no means ignore.
- P. We will serve the Lord gladly, for his service brings freedom.

23.
- L. The earth is the Lord's and the fullness thereof.
- P. We acknowledge God's ownership of our land and our lives.
- L. Our help is from the Lord.
- P. When we trust in him we will not be dismayed.

24.
- L. Come, let us rejoice, for God has set us free.
- P. He has given us back our lives so that we may live in peace and harmony.
- L. Let us praise God, for his love is unending.
- P. Our faith becomes effective when we allow ourselves to be channels of his love.

25.
- L. Praise the Lord, for his name is "Love."
- P. He has redeemed us. Though we have sinned, he has not turned away.
- L. It is not God's will that the wicked should perish.

P. We will seek the lost and tell them of your forgiving love.

26.
L. Welcome to the house of the Lord, the God of the Universe.
P. We stand in awe before his majesty and dedicate ourselves to his service.
L. Behold, this God whom you worship "will suddenly appear in his temple." Are your hearts prepared for such an encounter?
P. We are prepared to meet our God, for his boundless love sustains us at all times.

27.
L. The Lord has made known his victory.
P. He has revealed his vindication in the sight of the nations.
L. It is the God who said, "Let light shine out of darkness," who has shone in our hearts.
P. To give us the light of the knowledge of the glory of God in the face of Christ.

28
L. Stand fast in the Lord! Have no fear!
P. God is our refuge and strength, a very real help in times of trouble.
L. Do not be unnecessarily concerned about tomorrow, for God knows what we need.
P. We give our lives anew to him, to be used as he sees fit.

29.
L. Do not forget: The Lord our God is one!
P. He is a jealous God and demands our total allegiance.
L. Do not presume to say to yourselves: "We are God's people." "Bear fruit that befits repentance!"
P. We shall serve the Lord with all our hearts and minds, souls and strength.

30.
L. Come — worship the Lord our God, whose love upholds us even now.
P. He is our Lord and our helper — when we dwell in him we are at peace.
L. God is love, and when we make love our aim, God is with us.
P. Help us, Lord, to make our love genuine, so that we hate what is evil and love what is good.

31.

L. Come, worship the Lord your God with praising and singing.
P. We come joyfully to worship God!
L. God is Spirit.
P. And we must worship him in spirit and in truth, remembering always that we are called to love.

32.

L. Who are you?
P. We are children of God and brothers and sisters to one another.
L. What does it mean to be children of God?
P. It means worshiping God in everything we do, and loving and helping everyone we meet!

33.

L. Praise the Lord, for he is good!
P. O Lord, our God, how great you are!
L. Lord, you have granted us so many gifts, out of the greatness of your love for us.
P. We offer our words of praise and thanksgiving, and seek to follow them with our deeds of love and mercy.

34.

L. Arise and affirm the Lord our God.
P. We can trust the Lord to keep his promises.
L. "Seek the Lord while he may be found; call upon him while he is near."
P. We commit our lives to God. We shall put him first in all we do.

35.

L. There is one God and Father of us all.
P. "All who are led by the Spirit of God are children of God."
L. Come, walk in the way of the Lord, with songs of gladness and joy.
P. The Lord is near to us when we call upon him, but we must believe, and we must seek him in the right spirit.

36.

L. Let us lay aside every burden and every thought, however pleasant, which keeps us from serving God.
P. We commit ourselves to the living God and to Jesus Christ, who declared God's will to us.

L. God is love, and if we are his children, we will love one another as he loved us.
P. We open our hearts and our lives to everyone, and we pray that God will give us the courage to keep ourselves open.

37.
L. The world is new in Christ.
P. But only when we take up our lives in this world in his name.
L. Seek God where you are, not in airy sanctuaries of the mind.
P. We give our lives to God, even those humdrum moments which seem so unimportant.
L. In Christ, even ordinary moments take on a new glow,
P. And life is full of meaning.

38.
L. Come, take up your cross and follow our Lord.
P. But the cross is so uncomfortable and such a bother to bear.
L. Jesus said, "Take my yoke upon you, and learn from me, for my yoke is good to bear, and my burden is light."
P. OK, but you'll have to wait while we get a few things done first.
L. Jesus said, "Anyone who starts to plow and then keeps looking back is of no use for the kingdom of God."
P. So be it. We will follow God now.

39.
L. Come, let us worship the Lord with our whole being.
P. He deserves our very best efforts.
L. All that we have is from God, including our very lives.
P. We gladly live our lives as a gift from God and dedicate ourselves to his service.

40.
L. God, our Lord, uphold us now; here before your presence we bow.
P. We thank you, Lord, for being here; your love casts out our every fear.
L. We stand before your judgment seat and only ask your love to meet.
P. We walk in ways we know not of, content to be within your love.

41.
L. Come — worship the Lord who gives us the victory.

P. He lives, and because he lives we shall live.
L. Take up your cross and follow him who can turn that cross into a crown.
P. *We give our lives to God so that we may become new beings.*

42.

L. Come, let us join together in worshiping God, our Father.
P. *He is ready and able to give us every good and precious gift so that we may lead a good life.*
L. His love can set us free — if we will but open our hearts to him and to one another.
P. *We open our hearts so that the Lord may enter and make his temple there.*

43.

L. God is waiting to enter our lives.
P. *Let us open our lives to God.*
L. He will come to those who are ready for him, and they will find peace.
P. *Our hope is in the Lord. We will seek to follow his way.*

44.

L. We stand in the presence of God.
P. *He is in our midst; his truth supports us; his love guides us; and in mercy he forgives us.*
L. The Lord is our strength.
P. *In him we are able to stand; in his glory we see our destiny.*

45.

L. Know that the Lord our God is a loving God.
P. *He does not willingly punish us, nor will he desert us.*
L. Let us give as freely of ourselves as God has given himself to us.
P. *We will walk in God's way, for there we shall find joy and life.*

46.

L. You are the light of the world, and light is meant to be displayed, not hidden from view.
P. *We will not hide from our responsibilities; we will live in the open, lives befitting children of God.*
L. You are the salt of the earth, whose task is to bring joy, not drabness, to others.
P. *We will not allow ourselves to become dull and listless — we will rejoice in the Lord.*

47.

L. Why do you come here?
P. *To worship the one true God!*
L. And how are we to worship him?
P. *By giving of ourselves and by living as Christ showed us how to live.*

48.

L. Come, Lord, bestow upon us your presence.
P. *Create in us a clean heart, O God, so that we may better serve as your instruments for peace and love.*
L. We come into your presence so that we might be regenerated.
P. *Then we will be able to take up our task as your gift to a people in need.*

49.

L. Come and receive the new life Christ has promised.
P. *We gladly accept the gift so freely given.*
L. With thankfulness in our hearts let us face the coming days.
P. *With Christ as our guide and strength we can face anything.*

50.

L. Come, worship the Lord, for he is good, and you will find rest for your soul.
P. *We give our lives over to God, who is able to comfort us.*
L. Ours is the victory in Christ.
P. *Now we are prepared to take up our lives and live them in Christ's name.*

Prayers of Confession

1.

O God, as we begin this Advent season, we are all too aware of the hypocrisy in our lives, the shadowy areas which we are afraid to bring to the light of day. We have wronged your children, and thus we have wronged you. We have been too fearful to confront one another in love, and so we have allowed sins to persist within ourselves and others, sins which cause separations between us and them, between us and you. Forgive us, Lord. As we prepare ourselves to receive Christmas within our hearts, help us to learn to be honest and open in our dealings with one another. Give us the courage to confront others and ourselves with the necessity for laying aside all our petty presumptions which close our hearts to your presence. May our lives become a continual affirmation of your presence. Amen.

2.

O God, our Father, Redeemer and friend, our hearts are heavy with our sins. During this joyous season, we are in need of your presence, so that our eyes might be open to the needs of those around us. We confess that we are too quick to consider our duties done, and long before the battle for life is over, we convince ourselves that we have done our part. Convince us, O Lord, that our calling is open-ended, a never-ending commitment to be followers of Christ. Grant us the insight to be aware of our own deficiencies and the courage to take ourselves in hand, so that, when our life has ended, we shall stand redeemed. In Jesus' name we pray. Amen.

3.

We confess, O Lord, that we, who have received the greatest gift in creation, Christ, and the freedom to be ourselves and thus to commune with you, we, your children, have been guilty of failing to hope. We, who were given freedom, have chosen the bonds of tradition, preferring the comfortable shackles of what we know to the mystery of your presence. Forgive us our fears, God, which have prevented our reaching out to you and to one another. Inspire us, by your loving presence, to accept the freedom Christ offered us, to be open and courageous in our living. In Jesus' name we pray. Amen.

4.

O God, you have given us so much. In this Advent season we celebrate Christ's presence in our lives and prepare our hearts for your coming. Overlook our frailties, which so often blind us to your presence and to one another's needs. Forgive us when we live selfish little lives with little time for the needs of your children. Grant us the wisdom to see Christmas with the eyes of children, with awe and gratitude, so that our lives may take on a glow that will light up the lives of everyone we meet, and so that we may be worthy of fellowship with you, the universal God, whose name is love. Amen.

5.

L. God, you have given us so much to be thankful for. Even in the midst of trouble we feel your presence near.
P. *It sustains us so that we are able to affirm, with Paul, that nothing is able to separate us from your love.*
L. Yet we are not all that we could be. We hold back from giving every nook and cranny of our lives over to your loving care. We affirm that your way leads to life, but when times get rough, we fall back on our old patterns of behavior.
P. *We affirm your Lordship, but other people and other things often determine our behavior.*
L. Renew us, Lord. Cleanse our hearts of cowardice and self-concern. Forgive us our foolishness and lead us in the way we must go.
P. *We will follow, though hesitantly at times, and with your help, we will make this Advent time a time of renewal of faith, hope, and especially love.*

6.

O God, you have given us of yourself. You rejoice when we rejoice; you weep when we weep. Every sin of ours is like another nail driven into the flesh of Christ and into your heart. We have so much to be grateful for, yet, in arrogance, we shun you, while making selfish use of the gifts you have given us. Forgive us, God. Enable us to lay hold of the new life that is ours in Christ so that our lives may be joyful and abundant, and we may find that peace which passes understanding. Amen.

7.

God, we profess to love you, but we so often avoid you when there are tough decisions to make, because we know that which you will demand of us — that we base our decisions on justice and love. But we don't want justice — unless it means we get what we want. We don't want love — unless it means we are on the receiving end. Giving love and allowing justice to prevail are against our nature. We are taught to focus our attention on getting and on success, measured in terms of how much we can amass for ourselves. It is hard for us to change, God. Come into our hearts, so that we may shake off the shackles that bind us to selfishness and despair. Lead us to the true freedom which releases us for love and hope. Amen.

8.

O Lord, our God, our dim vision prevents us from seeing who we are. We ignore our past, especially when it is embarrassing, and yet we hold the past of other people against them. We ignore much of our present because we are unable or unwilling to admit our failures therein. We stumble into our future because we will not learn from our past, accept our present, or prepare for our future. Forgive us, Lord. Enable us, by your love, to be the frail humans we are to the extent of our ability. Open our eyes that we may see, our minds that we might think, and our hearts so that we may dare to live. Amen.

9.

Gracious Father, you are always willing to use us, in spite of our faithlessness. We confess that, while we have been chosen to live as servants, we have tried to be masters instead. Our Lord has given us the pattern of poured-out life, but we crave the successes, honors, and statistics which star us in bright lights. We have received a commission to be witnesses to the end of the earth, but in our self-interest, we devote our time to oiling the machinery of our own organizations and pet projects. We have closed our ears to the prophetic signs of our times. We lack the conscience that should accompany our Christian profession. Forgive us, O Lord, and deliver us from our living death. Give us the courage to accept the pain of new birth so that we may be renewed and healed from all our brokenness. Amen.

10.

O God, you have called us in love and to love, but, like your children of Israel before us, we have been at times lethargic and at times overzealous in your name. We seem to alternate between avoiding our responsibilities and taking upon ourselves responsibilities which belong to you alone. At times we say it doesn't matter what anyone believes, as long as they believe, and, at other times, we punish severely all those who dare to disbelieve what we believe. Forgive us, God. Teach us to value everyone we meet as a child of God. Grant us the courage to speak our convictions, but fill our hearts with your love so that we may always speak the truth in love. Amen.

11.

O Lord our God, you have granted us, as your children, a great freedom to create our world in your image, but often we shun the light of your truth for the comfortable darkness of our little caves. We sometimes become wedded to outmoded ways of living because they are comfortable, and we fear the discomfort that change can bring. However, in the process of trying to conserve our ways of life, we find ourselves at times transgressing and destroying values that our forefathers have achieved for us at great sacrifice. Heal our blindness, God; lead us by the light of your truth, so that we may see ourselves as we really are: free persons, endowed with great creative powers, if we will only use them in the way you meant for them to be used. In Jesus' name we pray. Amen.

12.

God, we confess that freedom frightens us. It is a great challenge to take the freedom that you offer us and use it creatively to bring about a new world. We find questions which seem too difficult for us to answer, tasks too difficult for us to perform. We become frightened, and in our fear, we seek an excuse to pull into our shells. We accept simple answers from people who are as frightened as we are. Remove our fear far from us, and enable us to accept ourselves, and others, as we are, with all our limitations. Give us the courage to accept this world, where questions outnumber answers, and give us the patience, which will enable us to settle for nothing less than the truth. Amen.

13.

O God, our Father, so often we despair and think the world is closing down around us. We seek serenity by escape from involvement. We try to ignore the problems of the world by retreating to our own little isolated homes and placing our faith in our own ability to survive. We do not take our covenant or our community seriously, or else we would turn to you and to one another for support. Forgive us, God. Help us to become your ambassadors to a world lost in sin. Give us the courage to preach your word of reconciliation to a world where people put their faith in punishment and seek to escape their own just blame by blaming others. When we are despondent, awaken us to the reality of your steadfast love. Amen.

14.

Our Father, often our hearing is dull when you would speak to us, and often our eyes are half blind when you would show us your way. Within the comfort of our homes, we often find ourselves entrapped by lethargy. We wish to know your will for us, but we wish others to take the responsibility of deciding for us. Forgive us, Lord. Lead us out of the morass of complacent thinking. Challenge us to take our fate within our hands and follow Christ. In Jesus' name we pray. Amen.

15.

O God, most merciful Father, we acknowledge that we have talked with unbridled tongues about one another, stretching the truth when it seemed "necessary" to control the unworthy. We have taken pride in our little groups rather than in the inclusive fellowship of Christ to which you have called us. We have put first our ideas of what you ought to be, and of what our relationship with you should be, rather than that love which knows no differences. Forgive us, O Lord. Teach us to respect one another and to put your kingdom before all other considerations, seeking with all our heart, mind, soul, and strength to accomplish your kingdom on earth. In Jesus' name we pray. Amen.

16.
O God, our guide and master, our lives do not always tell others of your loving presence. We often try to confine you to a corner of our lives, trying to control you, rather than turning our lives over to your control. We are more like self-willed children than self-giving adults in the area of expressing our faith in our lives. Forgive us, God. Bring to naught our self-willed endeavors so that we might know you as Lord of all life, and not just of a portion of life. Help us to become aware of the great gift and the great challenge which are ours: the gift of new life, and the challenge to live fully a Christlike life. Amen.

17.
O Lord God, we confess that we have too easily despaired in these trying times, losing confidence in your promise to be with us and to uphold us. We have, instead, confined ourselves to easy tasks, where we were certain of success, leaving the difficult task of ministering to this troubled world to others. Forgive us this cowardice and inspire us to seek and carry out your will, regardless of the difficulties involved. Amen.

18.
O God, we come to you in the knowledge that we have closed ourselves to one another. You call us to be open, but the pain and fear in our lives lead us to righteous indignation against those who sin against us. Help us, God, to realize that your love is sufficient for our lives, and if we will live in that realization, no words, or deeds, can really harm us. Give us the strength and the love to reach out to those who deny us their fellowship or who harm us in any way. Amen.

19.
O Lord God of the universe, we hear your call, but we are too complacent. We go about in our daily lives, politely ignoring the servants you have sent to call us to participate in your kingdom. For a trivial moment of pleasure, we let our birthright slip through our careless fingers. Forgive us, God. Teach us to examine ourselves and our world with an open awareness of your presence so that we may answer when you call. Amen.

20.
O Lord God, we acknowledge that our bodies are your temple, and that we are called to take care of our bodies so that we may not be prevented from rendering our fullest service to you. Despite this knowledge, we have abused our bodies, by failure to exercise properly and by taking drugs, which we often would

not need if we would but exercise our discipleship and our willpower to their fullest possibilities. Forgive us our weakness. Help us to realize our possibilities for Christian discipleship, so that our lives may be abundant and joyful. In Jesus' name we pray. Amen.

21.
O God, our gracious Father, we admit that we have often followed Christ only when it was convenient. We are tempted to force our will on others, and we are too subservient to people who have amassed a great deal of wealth and power. Rather than judging righteously and fairly, we judge our friends leniently and our enemies harshly. We toady to the rich and oppress the poor. We are the Pharisees of today, blindly holding on to our privileges and putting off the loving response that Christ has called us to. Forgive us, Lord. Open our eyes, so that we may see, our hearts, so that we might feel, and our minds, so that we may know that you are our God and we are your people. Enable us to live Christ-like lives, earnestly speaking the truth in love to everyone we meet. Amen.

22.
O God, even with your Spirit upon us, we tremble with fear when we encounter situations we cannot control. Rather than confront one another in love, we choose to hide from one another, pretending to believe what we do not believe and to feel what we do not feel. We hurt, but we won't admit it. Others hurt, but we pretend not to see. And so we live an unreal existence, hating ourselves for being phony, but unwilling to take the risk of authentic living. Be with us, God. Give us the courage to live for you and to reach out to one another in loving concern. May living for you be more important in our lives than all the plaudits of people, and may we be open and accepting of one another so that your Spirit may have full reign in our lives. Amen.

23.
O God, you are the one true God. Your love enfolds us; your wisdom guides us. We know that peace comes only from serving you, and yet we still allow fears and greed to blind us. We fear losing what we hold dear, so we abandon your way of love, gaining thereby the world but losing your presence, and hence our peace of mind. Forgive us our foolishness, Lord. Give us the courage to follow Christ's example of love, even when it means suffering or losing everything we have. Help us realize that life is

not worth living, and there is no future worth having, until we are willing to sacrifice our future in order to serve you. Amen.

24.

O God, in our egotism we often pretend to be better than we are, afraid that if we confess our weaknesses we will lose the love of those around us. We cannot really hide our sins, but we hope to avoid their consequences by ignoring them. Help us to realize that only as we lay aside our pretenses and deal with you and with one another as *real* persons can we accomplish your will for us and truly become a healing community. You love and accept us as we are. Teach us to love and accept one another as we are, so that we may accomplish good for all your children. Amen.

25.

O God, so often our ambition and our greed betray us! We desire to live with "gusto," and so we try to keep up with the "Joneses" by accumulating many possessions. Even when we seek a more "spiritual" existence within your church, we seem to be driven more by a desire for self-advancement than for loving service. Like James and John, we desire the "high places." We make a commitment to you, but we hedge our commitment about with vague words which enable us to continue living our selfish ways. Forgive us, Lord. Speak to us in a clear voice through your prophets so that we may recognize our narrow self-concern for what it is. Move us by your love so that we may attain to that life style that Christ demonstrated so well for us, a way of living that asks not "What's in it for me?" but "What would you have me do, Lord?" Amen.

26.

O Jesus, we behold you on the cross, and we worship from afar; but then we turn our backs and go our separate ways. When you come to us in our daily lives and call to us through the needs and hurts of others, we are deaf to your cry. We are good at making resolutions, but we fail to see the opportunities we have for carrying them out. We put you on a pedestal, and then we ignore you, except for ceremonial purposes, or when trouble threatens. We fail to see that you have called us to give over our *entire* lives to you, and we selfishly seek to have our salvation, and still hang on to our narrow-minded ways. Enfold us in your love, inform us with your wisdom, and challenge us in your gay abandon for God. We, too, would be like you — a people aflame with a purpose. Amen.

27.

Father, when we pray to you, we realize just how far we are from living the way Jesus called us to live. We see people starving, and we turn away. We see conditions which prevent people from accepting your existence, and yet we do nothing to change those conditions. Your name is honored by so few people, and even we forget to honor you at times, being more concerned, as we often are, with getting along with our neighbor than we are with pleasing you. Forgive us, God, and help us to be more forgiving. Inspire us by the example of Christ so that we may become more fully involved in bringing your kingdom closer to people and people closer to your kingdom. May our lives show forth the light that you have given us. Amen.

28.

O God, Christ called us to be lovers, not judges, of one another, and yet so many times we sit in judgment of people we have not bothered to learn to know. We are so quick to forget your command to love and to forgive whenever we feel that someone is a threat to us or to our community or church. We profess our faith to all who will listen, and then we turn our backs on those who need us and unjustly condemn people whose only sin is weakness. Forgive us for being so quick to judge the weak and so prone to praise those who use their strength to their own advantage. Give us love so that we may be more accepting, wisdom so that we may be more judicious in our actions, and courage so that we may live faithfully within a secular, unloving world. Amen.

29.

O God, we know that new life is ours when we turn to you. Your love is free to us, simply for the asking. The world, however, has taught us to value power and those things which we acquire by our own hand and by the use of power. We despise, or pity, or even fear, those who believe absolutely in the power of love. We are offered freedom, but we prefer the safety of conformity. We fear too many people to allow freedom to reign, and so we create structures which limit our freedom as much as they do those whom we fear. Help us break out of our narrow ways to the great expanse of freedom available to those who live by faith in your light. Amen.

30.

O God, our Father, we have your promise that you will always be near to us. We have had the audacity of presuming upon your kindness by refusing to listen and by being of an unrepentant heart — and then crying out that *you* have forsaken *us*. We have been blinded by our desires so that we have lived our lives in ways alien to your love, paying little heed to one another's needs, making only half-hearted attempts to bring in your kingdom. Forgive us, Father. Bring your love to fruition in our hearts so that we may be enabled to become instruments of your love. Amen.

31.

O Lord, God of the Universe, your dominion extends to the ends of the earth. Great is your name. All who know your name stand in awe before you. We confess that, in spite of our knowledge of your universal rule, we have often used religion to limit your influence rather than as an avenue for serving you. We have made false distinctions between "religious" and "secular," limiting "religious" to a nebulous realm of personal feeling, and granting to "secular" all those areas of power where things are happening. Then we can excuse ourselves when we fail to minister to people in the midst of life or turn away from those who are not "one of us" without feeling guilty. Forgive us, God. Grant us the wisdom to see the error of such limiting concepts, and the love to overcome all attempts to separate your love from anyone. Amen.

32.

Almighty God, we praise you for committing to the hands of your children the treasures of your creation: the wealth of the forests, the riches of the earth, the fertility of the soil, and the blessing of water, to use for your glory and our good. We confess that we have often been unmindful of and wasted your gifts. As we meet together to worship you, lead us to remember all your mercies; and grant us, we pray, true repentance and the desire to amend our ways, so that in all things we may honor and glorify you. In Jesus' name we pray. Amen.

33.

Lord of all that is and is to be, sensitize our sight that we may see what really is and understand what ought to be. We confess that often we see only what we want to see. We strike for more vacations and benefits while thousands are cold, diseased, and poverty stricken. We believe no one can starve in America, while children die of malnutrition in our cities. We speak of equal rights, education, and justice for all, but can not feel the frustration of overcoming prejudice of race or nationality. We think the world population should be controlled, but fail to support planned parenthood programs because they don't apply to us. We create technology but fail to control it. We enjoy the company of lively people but don't reach out to their loneliness. Help us, Lord, to see the inconsistency of our living, and the distortions of life wherein we become destroyers rather than creators. Have mercy. Amen.

34.

O God, source of our strength in times of trouble, our light in the midst of our darkest despair, we admit that suffering often turns us inward, away from you and from those around us. In the midst of our suffering, Lord, may we seek to comfort others, rather than to be comforted. In the midst of our despair, may our faith not only be sufficient to uphold us but may it also be a light and an inspiration to those around us. Bless our lives with your presence so that we may be instruments of your peace. Amen.

35.

O God, our Father, forgive our foolish ways, our lust after our own desires, and our lackluster pursuit of the rights of others. We so often fail you and Christ by following after those things which are dear to our own hearts. Help us, O Lord, to learn to put aside everything which stands between us and you, between us and other people. Teach us to lead renouncing and reconciling lives, ever reaching out the hand of love to all your children. Amen.

36.

O loving God, we do not measure up to such a love. When we compare our love to yours, we know that ours is lacking. We find it hard to love people who are different, especially people who are hostile to us. But when we behold your love for us, and how you love us even when we are unloveable, we are encouraged to begin again to seek to follow in Christ's way and to love others as you love us. Amen.

37.

You send us many visions of possibilities, Lord, but we refuse to change our ways. They are too comfortable, and the possibilities of life that we perceive are far too challenging. You call for such changes in our lives that we are afraid, and we linger in the comfortable shadows of our ignorance, fearing the bright light of your truth. Forgive our fears, O Lord, which rob us of the joy that comes in ministering to a world in need of caring souls. Enable us to see that only those who meet the challenges we face are heirs to that abundant life which transforms sorrow into opportunity for meaning. Fill our hearts with that love which transforms conflict into opportunity for fellowship, and give us the courage of our convictions to persevere against all trials or temptations. Amen.

38.

O Lord God, you have granted us your grace, not because of our deeds but because of your great love. We have been the recipients of a great gift, but we are in danger of losing it because of our unwillingness to share it. We have been satisfied with too little, and hence we are in danger of losing what little we have. Forgive us, God. Help us to learn from the example of Christ that fullness of life comes from living on the growing edge, rather than amid the security of conformity, that, as we dare to live fully, we will live more meaningfully. May we take the risks of real living in stride, thankful for the opportunity of bearing witness to the world as to who we are, and *whose* we are. Amen.

39.

O Lord our God, you offer us so much and yet, in our narrowness of vision we settle for so little. In our blindness we have chosen the chains of a narrow faith that promises us something for nothing — and costs us our souls. We have ignored the voice of your prophets calling us to account for our failure to act responsibly. We have suffered, but our suffering has not opened our eyes. We have missed the opportunity to be a real community. Forgive us, God. Awaken us to the abundant life which awaits those who seek you with all their heart and mind. Create in us a new heart so that we may create a new world. Amen.

40.

O God, we have not meant to sit back in judgment when we ought to be reaching out in love. We just seem to enjoy judging. It feels so secure to be someone else's judge. Then, too, we have been hurt reaching out to people who are not yet Christians, and whose lives are messy. We haven't been too successful in helping them either. They don't seem to want our help, or else they don't want it the way we are willing to give it. It's so frustrating. We've been taught to succeed, and it's so risky reaching out in love, so easy to fail. Help us to overcome our fear of failure so that we may reach out, regardless of the consequences. Help us to be loving people, as Christ was a loving person. Give us the courage to bear witness to Christ's love wherever we are. Amen.

41.

God, we have been told by Christ, by the Apostles, and by many others throughout our history that you love all people with a great, forgiving love. We often profess our joy at such a love, and yet there are so many times when our actions deny that we really understand your love. We seek to hoard your love for ourselves and our friends. We refuse to reach out to sinners *before* they have asked our forgiveness, knowing all the while that *you* reached out to us while *we* were still sinners. Forgive us, O God. Inspire us by your love so that we might be channels of love even to those whom we despise, lest we cut ourselves off from your love. Amen.

42.

O God, you have given us families in which we early learn to sing your praise, and you have given us the church where we find fellowship that strengthens us and enables us to find peace even in the midst of our troubles. Where would we be without you and without one another? But we are tempted, Lord, to "go it alone," to deny our need for one another, to look out only for ourselves. Thus we separate ourselves from our greatest source of your grace. In our pride of independence, we lose our dependable community, which is able to soothe our troubled brow. Forgive us our foolishness, Lord. Help us to see that there is a dependence on one another that gives us the strength to stand alone when we need to. And help us to be the kind of community that encourages growth and trust. Amen.

43.

O God, you gave us your love in Christ, a love which is able to renew us and to free us from all our petty fears. We, however, have been foolish enough to turn aside from your love, arrogantly trying to "make it on our own." In our foolish pride, we have pretended to be free precisely in those areas where we are most enslaved. We deny our dependence upon you and upon one another, for we see an expression of need as an admission of weakness. Forgive us, God. Help us to see the error of our arrogance so that we may become truly free within your community of love, the church. Amen.

44.

O Lord our God, your love enfolds us and makes the darkest night as light as the brighest day. We find rest for our souls when we abide in you, and yet we are so quick to forget your counsel. We become deadened to your presence by our worldly concerns. We set our hearts on certain things, and we employ any means to obtain them. We scoff at those who seek to call us back to responsible living, and, yet, when the day of calamity comes, we turn to you with full expectation of immediate help. We who will not help others, or even ourselves, want you to help us, and all this we expect without an ounce of repentance on our part. Forgive us our arrogance, Lord. Bring to naught our foolish plans. Give us ears to hear your prophets calling us back to your love. Awaken our hearts so that we may feel your presence near. Amen.

45.

O God, your love is forever. Even in our darkest moments, when our thoughts are farthest from you, your love reaches out to us, calling us back to our senses. Forgive us for being so hard headed and hard hearted that we refuse to accept the fact of your presence in those who confront us with problems that call for hard decisions. Forgive us for putting ourselves first and for refusing to share our abundance with those who have so little. Forgive us for tolerating intolerable situations. Lead us by your love so that we may not be afraid to experience pain, to see sorrow, or to share the burdens, as well as the blessings, of living in this world. Amen.

46.

O God, we sense your presence among us. You offer us new life, but we are too vain to stop what we are doing, even though we vaguely sense our acts are death, and not life-producing. We are too fearful to trust ourselves completely in your hands, and so we continue to seek for meaning and value, all the while shunning the one way to reach it — the cross. We don't have confidence in sacrifice because we are used to thinking in terms of success. We are unable to receive your gift of new life because we are unable to receive. We have been taught to value independence, and so the idea of being dependent, even upon you repels us. Forgive us, God. Grant us the courage to turn away from all that holds us back from serving you, for only in serving you can we hope to find life. Amen.

47.

O Lord God, we confess that at times we are numbered among the fainthearted, seeing only obstacles where there are opportunities, crises where there are possibilities. Forgive us, Lord, for our lack of vision. Help us perceive in the cross of Christ the power to tame a universe. Give us a sense of destiny as instruments of your holy plan of salvation, whereby sinners are transformed into saints, and suffering and sacrifice are harbingers of spiritual power. May we accept with Christian maturity our cross, giving up our childish dependency upon those weak powers of the world which try to entice us from your saving grace. Amen.

48.

O Lord God, our Father, help us to realize that you love us as we are, and that we are to love one another with the same love. We confess that we have been, by turn, frightened and arrogant. We have been frightened when we equated being a Christian with being perfect and realized that we were imperfect. We have been arrogant when we pridefully assumed that, since we were saved, we were in a superior position to others and had a right to sit in judgment over them. Forgive us, Lord. Help us to view others and ourselves in proper perspective, as fellow-Christians on a pilgrimage of growth in grace. Help us to be a mutually supportive community, so that, by some means, all may be saved. Amen.

49.

O God, we are your children, chosen by you for the high privilege of bringing in your kingdom, and yet we content ourselves with gazing into our mirrors with self-satisfaction. We are so proud of who we are that we are tempted to forget that Christ called us to a task and not simply to a self-perpetuating fellowship. So many people look to us for help that we grow fearful that there are not sufficient resources to meet all the needs we see. Give us the courage, Lord, to do the best we can, taking note of the hazards we face so that we may deal with them, but not allowing them to turn us aside. Support us with your love so that we can resist the temptation to turn back before we reach your kingdom. Amen.

50.

We long, O God, for simpler days, when we believe it was easier to sing your praise. But we forget what fools we were, who could not see where evil stirred. Our eyes were blind, but now they see, and yet we sorrow at being free. Help us, Lord, to cease to grieve for what was not as we believe. Help us see that life is here for those who cast aside all fear and trust in you to bring to pass your promise that you made at last. Teach us to use the life you give to help all people truly live, to know that now it's great to be alive, that peace does come to those who truly strive to know your will. And, as we grow, in wisdom and grace, may every clan and every race become as one, in harmony, by love at last made free. Amen.

51.

Eternal God, we are so quick to fight for lesser things, for material goods, for so-called "honor," and other things, and so slow to stand for justice and mercy. We treat our enemies with disdain or outright hatred, forgetting how Christ called us to love even those who harmed us. We appeal to the law of "an eye for an eye, and a tooth for a tooth," even though we know Christ called us to a higher way. Forgive us, Lord. Help us to follow in Christ's way, renouncing those violent solutions we are so prone to accept. Amen.

52.

O God, you created us so that we might have fellowship with you. You gave us minds to think with and hearts to love with, so that we might be worthy of fellowship with you, and so that we might aid you in creating your kingdom. You gave us feelings so that, like you, we might feel the pain of our sisters and brothers, and minister to them in their hour of need. But we have sought to dull our feelings, to curb our hearts and our minds, so that we might keep our responsibilities down to manageable proportions. We have sought to "dole" out our love to those who have proved themselves worthy of our love. But you don't limit your love, do you, Lord, not even to us when we are so miserly with ours. Forgive us, Lord. Help us to dare to stretch our souls, to live out our lives in suffering service, if need be, with hearts willing to face any task. Amen.

53.

O God, the Lord of our daily lives, we confess that we have often been too busy to serve you. We have failed to appreciate our possibilities for serving you and our brothers and sisters. When it comes to our Christian responsibilities, we often seem too quick to see our shortcomings and too unwilling to take advantage of the opportunities for learning that are presented to us. Help us, Lord, to realize that you want us now, with all our weaknesses and ignorance, to start serving you, to realize that now is the time for us to act, now is the day of salvation. In Jesus' name we pray. Amen.

54.

O God, you have given us many gifts, gifts that enable us to be cocreators with you of your kingdom on earth. When we use them wisely, our community becomes the Body of Christ to a world in need of witnesses to your saving grace. At times, though, we fail to appreciate the gifts you have given us, because they seem so insignificant in comparison with the gifts that others have. Fear, too, prevents us from doing anything that could cause us to stand out from the crowd. At other times, we take such pride in our gifts that we do not appreciate the gifts that others have, and our puffed-up pride creates chaos rather than community. Forgive us, when we fail to use your gifts properly. Inspire us to use them for the good of our community and for the good of the world, so that all people may come to know your saving presence. Amen.

55.

O God, our loving Father, you love us when we are unloveable and continually reach out to us, even when we repudiate you. Such a love demands of us that we love likewise, but we are content to remain in our little world, aloof and apart from those who need our love and understanding, even as we need yours. We read of the unmerciful servant who refused to forgive his fellow servant a small debt, even when his Lord had forgiven him a great debt — and yet we fail to see that we are the servant who was forgiven a great debt. Forgive our hardness of heart, Lord. Enable us to see Christ in our brother and to see everyone as our brother. Amen.

56.

O Lord God, your peace is available to all who in humility and love seek it. In your love we are made whole again, and life takes on meaning. Sorrow gives way to rejoicing, fear to hope. Your peace keeps our hearts free from the trouble surrounding us, so that we are more than conquerors in Christ who has shown us the way to your temple. We know that we are often victims of fear and are tempted to turn away from the path to life by those who are filled more with a feeling of self-importance than your Spirit. Strengthen us, Lord, so that our lives may be an example to those who are weak. Give us the courage to reach out when life seems darkest, the faith to believe when belief seems vain, for, in the power of your presence, we are indeed able to face any condition. Amen.

57.

O God, your Word burns in our hearts. We hear your call, and our hearts are stirred to follow where you would lead us. However, even our family and friends, at times, seek to call us away from your will for us at that moment, luring us to follow plans of their devising. We are consumed with anxiety about their reaction if we refuse to go their way. This anxiety sometimes causes us to participate in actions or programs we don't believe in. Forgive us, God. Teach us to place your love of us and your demand for our allegiance above all those other voices clamoring for our allegiance. In Jesus' name we pray. Amen.

58.

Eternal God, you have chosen us as your children, and yet we often fail to bear fruit that could prove us so. Our lives become encircled by countless cares and concerns, and we live out our lives in quiet desperation. We have but to reach out, and you are there, and yet we lose our way in the darkness of despair, or we glibly affirm a live-and-let-live policy which is unconcerned about the blind guides which so many people follow in our world today. Help us, God, to become your children indeed, so that we may help your light to enlighten the darkness of our times, your knowledge to melt away the ignorance of which so many are so proud. Above all, may your love enliven us so that we may live to the full this life you have given us. Amen.

59.

O God, when we consider the fearfulness with which we live, we are ashamed. Christ has set us free, and we live as slaves to our possessions. We become so protective of what we have that we forfeit the higher life that Christ promised to those who follow him. We want to live as Christ taught us to but it is difficult when our society demands our first loyalty. Forgive us for being timid. Open our eyes so that we may perceive your will for us in our daily lives. Encourage us by your presence so that we may conquer our fears and our possessiveness. Only then can we truly live and obtain that peace which enables us to dare for you. Amen.

60.

Lord, we are so like the Pharisees! We set out to hallow your name and wind up by crucifying Christ and all others who get in our way. So quickly our divine mission takes on demonic overtones, and pride of place, or love of power, entice us to become despots, demanding allegiance to *our* ways. We become so fearful of error that we squeeze the life out of the Gospel and make it an empty set of rules, rather than a guide to freedom and life. Forgive us, Lord. Instill your love within our hearts so that our labors of love do not become labors of hate, and so that we do not blind ourselves to your message of love by focusing our attention on points of insignificance. In Jesus' name we pray. Amen.

61.

O God, when we consider how you have given us life, we are grateful. You have entrusted to us the message of reconciliation, of your love freely given to all people, knowing that only when such responsibility is ours can it be truly said that we are your children. Yet we often take the easy way of waiting for someone else to do what is really our task. Forgive us, God; overlook our past failures. Do whatever is necessary to wake us from our slumber, encourage us to be about your business, and preserve our faith in the midst of adversity. Amen.

62.

O God, who confronts us all (even when we refuse to recognize you), awaken us from slumber and challenge us to answer your call. Forgive us when we hear but refuse to listen; when we have a word that needs to be said, but decline to speak; when we give in to the fear of people's reactions, and thus ignore the dictates of our conscience. Break through our cocoons of self-imposed security and show us what life and living as your people are all about. Amen.

63.

Lord, take away our blindness! Cure us of our inability to see what we look at. Too often we look about us but do not really see. We are blind. Help us to see the bad about us for what it is, rather than to turn away, and help us to see the beauty which surrounds us. We need your help so that our eyes might be opened and the wonders of life might become more real to us. Take away our blindness. Amen.

64.

All merciful God, our gracious Father, we cry yearningly for you to suddenly appear among us, but how are we to abide the day of your coming? We smugly expect it to be a day of joy and exaltation for us, unaware that it can also bring condemnation. In the name of piety, we set the standards for your coming to us. We demand splendor, majesty, and power, for that is what we truly worship. Forgive us, God, and remove the blindness from our souls, so that we may perceive your presence in the fragrance of the flowers and the stench of the ghetto, in the beauty of a sunset and the ugliness of a cold-water flat. Help us to learn that wherever people are, you are, calling us to find you, to find life. Amen.

65.

God, your love is unfathomable. We are never out of your sight or beyond your loving concern. You desire all people to live full and rich lives. We know this, and yet we hold back from attempting to realize your goals for all people. We excuse ourselves by calling the needy lazy or ignorant or worse. We blame others for the condition the world and society are in, and thus excuse our own actions or inaction. Forgive us, Lord, for tolerating evil in ourselves or others. Give us the courage and love we need to stand up for the truth so that our world will be a better place to live in. Help us to walk in the way Christ showed us to be your way: the way of love. In Jesus' name we pray. Amen.

66.

O Lord our God, you come to us in many ways and constantly call us to respond. Your Word is proclaimed in this fellowship of worship, but it is also present in the morning newspaper, in our place of work, our homes, in the music we hear. Indeed, your Word comes to us in all of life. It is present when we feel well and when we are ill or depressed; when we are filled with faith and when we are beset with doubt; when we are faithful and when we sin. Yet so often we shut our ears and our hearts to your Word. Forgive us, Lord, and help us to turn our hearts to you. Through Jesus Christ our Lord. Amen.

67.

O God, you have blessed us with your presence, a creative presence which makes new people of us. In your presence, we are able to live productive and meaningful lives. We are able to make a mark for ourselves as a "chosen people." So often, however, we miss our opportunity through laziness or through greed, seeking to find an easy way to power and glory. No longer content to serve the living God, we follow after gods of our own choosing, gods who give us fame and fortune but leave us empty. Forgive us our foolishness, Lord, and fill our emptiness with your Spirit, so that we may know the fullness of your grace. Challenge us to remove ourselves from vain pursuits and to follow in the way of the cross, a way that often leads through hardship, but the only way that leads to life. Amen.

68.

O Lord, our gracious Father, we seek your will for us, but when that will leads to a cross, we often discover that we are too "busy." We excuse ourselves by saying that we do not want to "hurt our friends," or that we need to be "diplomatic," or that "change takes time." What we really mean is that we can't stand the pain that being your children often involves. Forgive us, God, and enable us, by your grace, to overcome our cowardice and to take up our crosses and bear them to your glory so that all walls of hostility may be broken down and all may live in harmony with one another. In Jesus' name we pray. Amen.

69.

O God, you come to us gently and quietly, like a vision in the night. Your presence lights up our lives and gives meaning to the smallest task. When we turn to one another in compassion, we experience your compassion for us in a thrilling way. However, Lord, we must confess that mighty miracles often get more attention in our religion than the little acts of compassion that you expect us to perform. People pay more attention to us when we do something extraordinary. Therefore, we are tempted to "play God," and give the people what they want. Help us to realize, Lord, that a cup of water given in your name is more important than any great miracle, that our everyday acts of compassion to those who are suffering and sorrowing do more to forward your kingdom than flashy miracles. Amen.

70.

O Lord, Almighty God, hear our prayer. In our concern for our daily needs, we often forget our rich heritage which has made us what we are. We are falsely puffed up with the notion that we have delivered ourselves by our own right hand, and we refuse to acknowledge our dependence upon you and upon the many others, the fruits of whose labors we enjoy. Forgive us, Lord, for our selfish blindness, which asks only of life: "What's in it for me?" Help us to see that only as we fully participate in life and take up the torch of faith and pass it on, do we find salvation. Amen.

71.

We are comfortable building walls, Lord, with the idea of live and let live, with the thought of "protecting our own." It's when we read your radical demands that we have trouble, especially when you tell us that the only way to find true life is to give up this life that has come to mean so much to us. It is difficult for us to let go of our "safe" world and venture into the unknown world to which you call us. Forgive us our timidity, Lord. Inspire us by the examples of Christ, who would not turn aside, even from the cross, and of Paul, who considered that the sufferings brought on by service to you were not worth comparing to the joy of serving you. May we, like them, give of ourselves so that the joy of a life lived in love and devoted to you may become part of our experience. Amen.

72.

O Lord our God, we are so quick to avail ourselves of your grace, and so slow to submit our lives to your judgment. We wish to be self-indulgent and yet to be rewarded as if we were self-giving. We attempt to evade our responsibilities by engaging in bad theology, which excuses our laziness. We choose to ignore your living Word wherever it contradicts our desires. Forgive us, Lord, and teach our hearts to value love above all else, so that we may stand before you unafraid. Enable us, by your love, to live in such a way that we need never be ashamed of who we are or how we live. Amen.

73.

O Lord God, we believe — help our unbelief! Although we know that you are a God of love, it is difficult for us to live our lives in light of that knowledge. We are so quick to abandon our faith and use methods incompatible with it. We do not trust you, or ourselves, sufficiently to hold on to your way in the midst of this corrupt world. We quickly abandon your way and adopt the way of the world, when we find it expedient to attain an end devoutly desired. We acknowledge also, Lord, that we are more prone to accept the status quo, with its present satisfactions, than we are to commit ourselves to the uncertain future to which you call us. Forgive us, Lord. Help us to grow in wisdom and in faith, so that we may have the courage to follow the way of love, regardless of any discouragement which may beset us in our lives. Amen.

74.

O God, our gracious Father, you have offered us life, yet we often choose death. You sent your Son that we might learn how to have victory over death — and we crucified him because we could not bear his words or follow his example. Teach us that victory only comes from living fully. Forgive us when we choose instead to hide from life in fear of the cross that living fully may bring. Help us to realize that each time we refuse to bear our cross we crucify Christ anew, and inspire us by your Spirit so that, when your call comes, we will answer enthusiastically and without reservation. In Jesus' name we pray. Amen.

75.

God, we complain when things don't go our way. Often we accuse you of forgetting us and leaving us alone. You are as near to us as prayer, but when we pray, we often ask of you benefits which we can only have at the expense of others, who are also your children. We get so busy that we don't have time for those things which are important to you. We don't take time to consider who we are and what tasks you may have for us. Forgive us, Lord. Help us to see how much we are missing when our minds are not stayed on you. Teach us to value what you value, so that our lives may take on meaning. Above all, help us to see that we are thrice blessed when we reach out in love, for thereby we find community and ourselves. In Jesus' name we pray. Amen.

76.

O God, children are especially dear in your sight, and yet we have tolerated a great deal of unnecessary pain and damage to children. Too many children go without proper clothing and shelter. Too many are hungry and ill. Our efforts to help are often too little and too late. It is too easy to evade our responsibilities and too hard to deal with the problems, so we escape behind a torrent of words, speaking our concern but not living our concern. Forgive us, Lord. Open our eyes that we may see and give us the love and courage to act so that all children may know the blessing of belonging to a caring community. Amen.

77.

O God, your name is love, and you have loved us with a love beyond our understanding, because, in your love, you have not condemned us, nor deserted us, even when our sins were greatest. But we not only fail to understand your love, we are unable to be loving to others. We especially find it difficult to love sinners, even though you have forgiven us our sins and have challenged us to forgive the sins of others. In our pride, we mistake shadows for reality, and vaunt things that are passing over your eternal love. Forgive us, Lord. Grant us the courage to seek wisdom and the even greater courage to follow wisdom where it leads. Above all, enliven our hearts so that we may learn to love each other. In the name of Jesus, your Son and our Savior, we pray. Amen.

78.

O Lord, our God, in whose eyes we are all important, we confess we have sought to dominate one another. Often we have professed to honor others when, in actuality, we were attempting to force them to play a role we expected of them. We have allowed ourselves to get caught in a vicious circle of mutual manipulation. We have forgotten that all people are created in your image and thus created for freedom. Enable us to allow everyone to be free, for only then will we find the abundant life waiting for those who are free and who allow others to be free. Amen.

79.

O Lord God, our gracious Father, we know that our haphazard way of keeping your Sabbath is painful to you. Often we have mocked your Sabbath by placing unnecessary burdens on people, preventing your healing grace, and often we have profaned your Sabbath, seeking not your presence but our own joy. Forgive us, Lord. Show us the error of our ways, and lead us to true repentance, so that we may live rejoicing and redeeming lives. In Jesus' name we pray. Amen.

80.
O Lord, you gave us minds to seek your truth, but we, through laziness or selfishness, use our minds instead to create idols that excuse the comfortable way we have chosen to live. Forgive us our negligence, Lord. Inspire us to become seekers and speakers of truth, so that we, and our world, may come to know the way that leads to life. Amen.

81.
God, you have given us many gifts. Through proper use of these gifts we grow, and our church grows. But, too often, we use our gifts for our own advancement, without caring what happens to those whom we do not know. We look out for "number 1" and excuse ourselves by saying that "everyone does it." Forgive us our selfishness, Lord. Cleanse us with your love so that we may learn to trust one another and to be trustworthy. Lead us in paths of love so that we may bring harm to no one and joy to many. Teach us to treasure the world we live in so that we may pass it on in entirety to our children. In Jesus' name we pray. Amen.

82.
O Lord God, our gracious Father, you guide us when we trust in you, and bring us safely to your side. With Paul, we can know that no situation can overwhelm us, for you will guide us and uphold us in the midst of our troubles. No path is too long, no night is too dark, when we follow you. But, Lord, we must admit that there are many times when we listen more willingly to our society's alluring voice than we do to your gentle prompting. We become so much a part of our culture that we fail to see the fallacy of its reasonings or the prejudices that so often prompt our behavior. Forgive us, Lord, for failing to listen. May our hearts and minds become attuned to your Spirit so that our lives may be a blessing to everyone we meet. Amen.

83.
Eternal God, we confess that we have often failed to serve you, sometimes out of cowardice, sometimes through laziness, and sometimes because of apathy. At other times, we have served you, but in such a grouchy way that others who saw us did not glory in your name but merely wondered why anyone would perform such an unwelcome task. Forgive us, Lord. Help us to know the why and wherefore of our service so that we may serve you with joy and gladness. In Jesus' name we pray. Amen.

84.
Lord God, we have abused your gift of life through selfish

disregard of others. We have lived fleshly lives of self-conceit and selfishness. We have not led lives of the Spirit, lives of love, care, and concern, for self and others. If we truly knew whereof we were born, we would so live that your Spirit would be obvious in our daily living. Forgive us, Lord. Inspire us to reach out to one another in forgiveness and love so that we may be fully your children. In Jesus' name we pray. Amen.

85.

O Lord, we confess that our tongues have been sharp and our hearing dull. We have sought our own way without listening well to others. We have too quickly judged what we didn't understand. Forgive us, God, and cleanse us of such narrow living. Enable us, by your love, to accept others, to accept our limits and our possibilities so that we may create a haven of peace where all people may come to an awareness of your presence and your love. Amen.

86.

O God, our gracious Father, whose name is "Love" and whose Spirit is "Truth," we stand before you with open eyes and do not see; your presence fills our lives, but our dull senses do not perceive; your call is clear, but our ears will not hear. Forgive us, our Lord. Inspire us to greater heights of endeavor than we have attempted, lest we allow the splendor of the light of your Son to fade before our desire-dimmed eyes. Encourage us to persevere in our Christian calling lest our fears lead us to sell out to a status quo which has little time for great things. Lead us, kindly light, so that we may find our way through the darkness which envelops us. In Jesus' name we pray. Amen.

87.

O God, you have created us, and you have made us inferior only to yourself, giving us dominion over all your works. With all the world at your command, you chose, instead, to trust in us. But, little by little, we have betrayed that trust. Our greed for gain and our fear of failure have tempted us to circumscribe your power and love. We glibly reason away our responsibility to create your kingdom here on earth. Help us, Lord, to open our hearts and our eyes as we read your Scriptures and study your world. Encourage us as we encounter obstacles to your will so that we might persevere in the face of many dangers and thus come to participate fully in your love. In Jesus' name we pray. Amen.

88.

O God, you have given us so much. Our lives are filled to overflowing. We have your promise of life, and we are a part of your community, which helps make this possibility a reality in our lives. If at any time we fail to live up to the best that is in us, or if we forget, at times, to reach out in love to one another, forgive us, and guide us back into your way of love. Teach us to care for one another, and for everyone we meet so that, one day, the whole world may come to see that in you we find life. Amen.

89.

Almighty and merciful Father, we greet this day as yet another opportunity to live and to love. Help us to make the very most of it, Lord, for life is too short for us to waste even this one day. We acknowledge and confess that we have in the past sometimes left undone those things which we ought to have done, and we have done those things which we ought not to have done. Forgive us for our past failings, Lord, and grant us new visions for this day and for all of the days which lie unexplored before us. Amen.

90.

Lord, we know that celebration plays too little a part in our lives. We often choose to let our thought dwell on what we lack and overlook the many treasures which are ours. Help us to be thankful for what we have. Teach us to let gratitude exemplify our daily lives so that we may be gracious rather than griping in our dealings with those around us. Amen.

91.

O God, we are your church. Throughout the ages you have been active in your church, making friends of enemies and preparing your people for ministry. Through the church we have learned of you, and through the church we have grown into the people who stand before you now. We have problems, but we are still able to share your gifts with one another and with our world, which stands so in need of your unchanging grace. We know that we do not measure up to your expectations for us, but we commit ourselves to the task of seeking your will for us and of being Christ to one another. Lead us, Lord, by your gracious presence. Amen.

92.

Eternal God, creator of the universe and of our lives, you have chosen us and called us out from the world to be a great people in your name, and you have given us the task of going back into the world to proclaim your name and your love. But we have chosen to enjoy your presence rather than to proclaim it, to lay claim to your love without sharing it. Forgive us, Lord. We have not realized that you did not call us to be spectators but missionaries. Inspire us by your presence so that we may have the strength and the courage to carry your message with us wherever we may go, if it be to the ends of the earth, or simply to the grocery store. Let all we do proclaim the majesty, power, and forgiveness of your presence. Amen.

93.

Lord God, our gracious Father, you would have us worship you in spirit and in truth, but we often shut out the Holy Spirit and seek to realize our own selfish ends. We are always tempted to use worship to coerce your grace or to realize our own desires. Often we shut our ears and hearts to our brothers and sisters and even to those in the worship service with us. Our justifiable concern for the state of our souls betrays us into selfish disregard for the souls and bodies of others. Forgive us, Lord, and help us to recover the vision which Christianity offers to us, the vision of freedom in love. In Jesus' name we pray. Amen.

94.

O God, our gracious Father, you have promised us new life, and we know that you carry out your promises. You have committed yourself to our well-being, and we know that, if we will turn and follow you, our lives will take on meaning and zest. But we are too comfortable in our little world, Lord. We like that which is familiar and predictable, and you often lead us along dark paths infested with thorns. We are afraid we might get hurt, and so we choose the comfortable little world we are familiar with over the unpredictable world you seem to call us to. Forgive us if we hesitate, Lord. Give us the courage and the wisdom to follow you, for darkness in your presence is to be preferred over seeming light when you are not there. In Jesus' name we pray. Amen.

95.

O God, giver of joy, in the midst of our problems, we seek to find the joy of your presence, for we know that only in you can our hearts find rest and that joy we seek. So often, however, we seek to find you apart from the problems of the world, for they are many, and they threaten to overwhelm us. And yet, Christ and Paul, and many others, have told us that we are to find you, and joy, in the midst of life, not in escape from life. Forgive us our selfishness and our fears, Lord. Teach our hearts to love, in order that we might live, and our minds to seek, in order that we might find that perfect peace of those whose lives are lived where you are: in the midst of your people. Amen.

96.

Eternal God, you have given us your Word to lead us in paths that strengthen our lives and our communities. In times of sorrow, your Word comforts us. In times of trouble, your Word challenges us to leave our comfortable little firesides and venture into the outer darkness, taking with us only the knowledge that you are with us. Help us, Lord, so that we may learn to trust in your presence, and in your way, even when we cannot see that your way will bring the results we desire. Forgive us when fear takes hold of our hearts and causes us to follow blind leaders who promise us what we want to hear. Give us the courgae to answer when you call: "Here am I, send me." In Jesus' name we pray. Amen.

97.

O God, giver of so many gifts, including the gift of life, we thank you for your generosity. Your love is beyond our understanding. You love us so much that you refuse to shackle our souls, even when we turn away from you. And yet, we are so quick to form shackles for others, demanding that they assent to our doctrines before we will grant them freedom or fellowship. We even demand perfection of ourselves, and seeing that such is not possible, we often retreat into our own private world. Forgive us, God. Give us the courage to take up our lives, with all their ambiguity, and live them in the light of the best we know. Amen.

98.

Eternal God, our light in a darkened world, you have created light out of the darkness of our lives and led us from the wilderness of sin. In your light we see life in all its glorious possibilities. We gladly worship you, but you desire more than our worship. You call on us to let your light shine through our lives, so that others may be brought into your kingdom. You have been gracious to us, and we should be glad to bear witness to your light. Instead, we cover it under a bushel. We hold back for fear of ridicule and for fear of hostility. People do not see your light because we give into our fears. Forgive us, Lord, and challenge us to leave our shells, lest we lose our lives by trying only to save ourselves. In Jesus' name we pray. Amen.

99.

O God, you have loved us from the beginning of our days, and we know that we can count on your love to the end of our days. We may turn from you and seek other gods, but you never turn your back on us. You are always offering us new lives for old, peace in place of poverty of Spirit, joy in place of sorrow, meaning where only emptiness prevailed. May your presence inspire us to take up our cross so that we may evermore live in an awareness of your life-giving presence. Amen.

100.

O God, our Savior, our hearts are heavy with the realization that we have used and abused our fellow human beings. We have not sought to root out our sins from within us. Rather, we have sought to cover our sins under a seeming righteousness, pretending to be what we are not. We have sought to evade just blame for our actions by laying unjust blame on others. Forgive us, Lord. Cleanse our hearts so that we might really become slaves of righteousness rather than mere pretenders. Amen.

101.

O God, you are so near — as near as our neighbor, and yet we so often live lives of quiet desperation because we do not listen to the whispers of your Spirit within our lives and our hearts. We search for you on mountaintops and miss your presence in our homes or at work because we are too wrapped up in things close at hand to hear your still, small voice. Open our eyes and ears so that we may hear you speak to our hearts, and so that we might see the tasks you lay before us. Amen.

102.

O Lord God, our gracious Father, you have begotten us in the midst of our lives — you have called us out from our narrow little worlds, so that we might live as a people set apart with you in our midst. We are often tempted to return to the quietude of our former ignorance, and we often yearn for a moratorium on our responsibilities. Maintaining our covenant with you, and showing others that they, too, are included in this covenant, is a monumental task, far beyond our poor powers. Come to us now, Lord. Empower us by your presence, so that we may meet our responsibilities and go on in power to perform the tasks you have given us, thereby finding the life you have promised us. Amen.

103.

O God, our Father, giver of life and our mainstay in the midst of strife, we acknowledge that false gods often hold an allure for us that they would not if we would but center our lives in your abiding presence. We have faith in you, but not enough, so we put most of our faith in our military might. We have hope because of you, but not enough, and so we put our hope and trust in plans of our own devising. We love you, but not enough, and so we tacitly support repressive laws and institutions, instead of reaching out in love to the lost and lonely. Forgive us, O Lord. Enable us to live affirmative lives, for only such lives are fitting of followers of Jesus, your Son and our Lord. Amen.

104.

Eternal God, we thank you for your many gifts, gifts which are beyond our understanding. We only know that, when we place our trust in you, we are able to do many things we would have thought impossible. We know that, at times, we have used these gifts for our own advantage and advancement. We have also failed to use them on many occasions, and on other occasions, we have called other people's gifts into question without sufficient reason. Forgive us when we take more pride in ourselves, as gifted persons, than we do in using our gifts for the benefit of many people. Create in us a love that finds joy in reaching out and a purpose in creating love where hate has reigned. Amen.

105.

O God, you have given to us so freely of your love, and you have guided us in the past when we went astray, or when we became hopelessly lost or confused. You are ever near, but the world is even nearer, and we are tempted to turn aside from the way you would have us go. The world counsels us to take the "easy way," and we think, "Why not?" We do not wish to upset anyone, so we are careful about what we say or do, not realizing the evil we are committing. Forgive us, God, for refusing to give you first place in our lives, for refusing to follow where you lead. May we learn to value your presence and your will for us more than we value anything else, including our own security. Amen.

106.
O Lord, you have prepared a place for us, and you come to us to show us the way to your promised land. However, we are so afraid of the vast desert that surrounds us, or else we are so pleased with the tiny oases that we have created with our own hands, that we will not follow you. Through fear or through pride, we choose a half life, filled with fear, in preference to the full life, filled with freedom and joy, that you hold out to us. We make a pretense of listening, but it's strictly for looks and short on action. Forgive us, Lord. Enter our hearts this day, so that we may dare to drink from the waters you provide and follow the paths that you have made, regardless of how thorny they may be. Help us to attain that peace that you give to all who dare to follow you. In Jesus' name we pray. Amen.

107.
O Lord God, Christ declared your forgiving presence is available to all who seek you and who endeavor to follow your will. We confess that, while we have sought you, we have not sought you with all our hearts, minds, souls, and strength. While we have endeavored to follow your will, we often are slow in responding to you, and at times we let our selfish desires prevent us from reaching out to you and to others. Forgive us our narrow vision, God. Inspire us by your presence to live out our lives in service to all people, as Christ has commanded us to do. Amen.

108.
O God, our gracious Father and Sovereign Lord, you have given us eternal life and have forgiven our sins. When we choose to follow in the way that your Son, Jesus Christ, showed to us, we find peace and joy filling our lives. All our troubles seem so small alongside our many blessings. However, at times we don't do so well at recognizing your presence in our lives. We get into comfortable ruts and expect you to encounter us only in the ways you came to our ancestors. When you come upon us unexpectedly, we often fail to recognize you. Forgive us our narrowness of vision, Lord. Open our eyes so that we may see and our hearts so that we may feel your presence near, and guide us as we seek to follow your way to the eternal life that you have promised. Amen.

109.
Almighty Yahweh, Lord of the mountains and the seas, we come before your presence with contrite hearts, for we know that we

have not lived as completely for you and for others as we ought to have lived. We have a narrow circle of friends to whom we reach out often. And we do reach out to others in our community and throughout the world on occasion, but we are not perceptive enough to the needs in our world — not even of our close friends. Forgive us, God. Help us to become aware of the needs around us. Help us to love, until love becomes so much a part of us that we cannot help but reach out to one another. In Jesus' name we pray. Amen.

110.

O God, our gracious Father, we are so anxious for our own welfare that we seldom have the time or energy to be *really* concerned for others. Our society has conditioned us to think first of ourselves and only then of others. By the time we have assured the necessary material blessings for ourselves and for our children, we don't have the time to serve others in any significant way. Forgive us, Lord, for getting our priorities so mixed up. Make us aware of the lesson that Jesus tried to teach us — that those who seek their life shall lose their life, and those who lose their life for your sake will find their life. Help us to learn that life is ours when we forget self and seek you in our neighbor. In Jesus' name we pray. Amen.

111.

O Lord God, our loving Father, we know who we are, and yet we often act like something other than what we are: your children. We know that we ought to reach out in love, and yet we try to coerce others to go in the way in which we wish them to go. We know that we are called to forgive, and yet we harden our hearts to one another. We know that we are called to seek you, and yet we allow you to speak to us only in ways that are familiar to us. Forgive us, God. Teach us more fully who we are and enable us so to live that no one will doubt that we are indeed your children. In Jesus' name we pray. Amen.

112.

O God, we have been so enslaved to our own passions and desires that we have been unable to hold out our hearts and our hands to you and to our brothers and sisters in Christ. Instead of loving them, we have cursed them and accused them of all manner of evil, when their only sin was disagreeing with us. Forgive us. Enter our hearts and cleanse us of all unrighteousness so that we may be enabled, by your grace, to live full and abundant lives, lives full of love and joy. Amen.

113.

O God, you have blessed us with your presence so that the roughest places seem smooth. In our darkest hours, we have but to turn to you to find comfort. Crosses become challenges, and hopelessness is swept away by the great love that you have for us. Forgive us when we are too blind to see, too heartless to care, that love conquers all obstacles. Give us eyes to see clearly our world in all its complexity and courage to care, even when caring causes us to suffer. Amen.

114.

We thank you, God, for your guidance through the dark valleys of our lives. People often conspire against us to force us to follow the world and its narrow-minded concern for the few and its neglect of the many, but your presence gives us the strength to stand for justice. Forgive us when we waver before the onslaught of those who try to convince us that the world's way is the right way. Give us the courage to stand fast, even when friends turn against us. Amen.

115.

Eternal God, our Father and our Lord, you have opened the portals of heaven to us so that we might live in your presence. You sent your Son to us so that we might know the way to true life, but we are sorely tempted to settle for less than the best. We admire those whose lives show the love and compassion that you feel for people of every description. In our own lives, we turn away from those who are different or dirty, forgetting that Christ called us to ministry and to authentic love, which does not desire but gives. Forgive our hardness of heart, Lord. Fill our lives with your Spirit, so that we might begin to live lives rich in your presence. In Jesus' name we pray. Amen.

116.

O God, Lord of life and truth incarnate, we humbly ask your forgiveness of our arrogance and self-conceit, which leads us to place our thoughts above your thoughts, our ways above your ways. We quickly forget the lesson of love which Christ taught and substitute for it the love of friend, but the hatred of enemy. We quickly abandon the road to truth because it would mean giving up cherished notions, and that we cannot do, Lord, not even for you. Forgive us our wanton self-regard, Lord, and teach us to value, and treat with dignity, everyone we meet. Give us the courage to pursue the truth, wherever it may lead; and grant that we may follow in your pathway all our days. Amen.

117.

Eternal God, our loving and gracious Father, you have promised us abundant life. You commissioned Jesus to proclaim that abundant life to us. He personified your care and concern for all people, no matter how insignificant a person might appear to be, and went to the cross, rather than betray his trust. We have his example to follow, but, while our words have proclaimed our obedience, our actions have often betrayed a lethargy and a self-concern which do not work your will for us, or for this world which is so full of sin and so much in need of our witness and concern. Forgive us, O Lord. Help us to measure up to your expectations for us, so that we may indeed find the abundant life you have promised. Amen.

118.

O God, our loving but sovereign Lord, you call us to leave our beds of fear and pain and walk the paths that lead to your kingdom. We hear your word of promise and know that there is a rainbow at the end of the storms that threaten us, but fear overpowers our hearts, and we hesitate before the dark journey into night of a future we do not see clearly. We want assurances of painless travel along familiar shores, but you call us to brave painful travel along foreign shores. Give us the courage to go forth into the unknown, to walk the dark valley of the shadow of death. Then we will know ourselves to be children of the most high God and will experience the peace that comes from following you. Amen.

119.

O God, you are a God of joy, and you desire a life filled with joy for us, your children. Through fear or pride, we often deny ourselves and others this joy, which you desire for us. We close our hearts to others, refusing to admit our dependence on, or debt of gratitude to, them. We have ignored our many blessings, preferring instead to remember our sorrows, so that we might indulge in self-pity. Teach us, Lord, to reach out to one another and to accept one another, for only then will we be able to perceive the power we have, as a community, to deal creatively with life in a way that will maximize joy and minimize sorrow. Amen.

120.

O Lord God, our gracious Father, we desire to be fully present to you and to one another, and yet we are unwilling to really be ourselves. We hide behind masks, fearful of being rejected by you and by those around us. We run from controversy because we are afraid our fellowship is not strong enough to stand the stress of being honest in expressing our beliefs and our feelings. Help us, Lord, to accept our humanity, our failings and our strengths. Help us to have enough confidence in you and in ourselves to live our lives according to the truth as we see it. Amen.

121.

O Lord, God Almighty, creator of the universe, we acknowledge your lordship over us. We confess, however, that the lure of false gods has often tempted us sorely, and, at times, has caused us to break our covenant with you. The sweet talk of soothsayers has deafened us to the clarion call of your seers, and we are often tempted to give ourselves over to falsehood. Forgive us, Lord. Open our ears, that we may hear your prophets and be saved from the pursuit of those idols which are so satisfying to our palates but so destructive to our souls. In Jesus' name we pray. Amen.

122.

Ever-living God, by whose mercy we have come to the gateway of another year: Grant that we may enter it with humble and grateful hearts; confirm our resolution to walk more closely with you in your way, and to labor more faithfully in your service. Let not the errors and offenses of the past cling to us, but pardon and set us free, so that, with purer purpose, and a better hope, we may renew our vows in your presence, and set forth under the guidance of your Spirit to travel the path which shines ever more and more brightly for those who have eyes to see, ears to hear, and hearts to follow. In Jesus' name, we pray. Amen.

123.

Eternal God, Creator and Lord of the Universe, we marvel at the fact that we are your chosen people. You have guided us throughout our history, through epic events and through prosaic events. You have spoken to us through many gifted prophets, and even through your beloved Son, Jesus Christ. And yet, we have the audacity to pretend that your will for us is too difficult for us to determine. We deny you dominion in our daily lives, despite the biblical accounts which assert that your lordship is over *all* of life. But still, we profess concern for the Bible. Forgive us our arrogance, O Lord, and teach us to place you at the center of our lives. In Jesus' name we pray. Amen.

124.
O God, our gracious Father, what have we done to your love? It ought to bring us joy, but we often view the tasks you have for us as joyless. It ought to fill us with zest, and yet we often are listless and tranquil. It ought to fire us with a divine discontent with what is and a yearning for your kingdom, and yet we are too often satisfied with the present and seek to assure its continuance, by the use of despotic power if necessary. Forgive us, Lord. Inspire us to joyfully and enthusiastically affirm life and to seek your kingdom, rather than our own power and prestige. Amen.

125.
O Lord God, our lives lie open before you, and though we realize this, we find it difficult to live our lives in terms of this awareness. We are too easily blinded by our ambitions and our fears. Christ has set us free, but we trade our freedom for the security of sameness. We flee from the challenge of your presence, for we are not ready for the sacrifices which you demand. Forgive us, Lord. Show us the error of our ways and enable us to find that life which is full of meaning because it is centered in you. Amen.

126.
We are aware, God, of gaps in our lives, of places we protect from your presence, afraid to turn ourselves over completely to your keeping. We do not examine our lives or our situations as well as we should, because we don't want to face the truth that we are less than we ought to be, or that our situations are different than we want to see them. Forgive us our foolishness, settling for less than the truth of your presence, for preferring the darkness of our thoughts to the light of your truth. Free us from the dungeons of our design, from the shackles fashioned by our ignorance. Give us the courage to live in these days, when nothing is guaranteed but the power to live our days in your presence, knowing that nothing, not even death, can separate us from your love. Amen.

General Prayers

1.

We have begun to live for you,
  and with your help, O Lord,
we will continue in your love.
  Abide with us this day,
and lead us by the precious love
  that Christ has shown to us,
that love which never turns aside
  till closing of the day.
May we, like those who went before,
  live our lives for you,
so at the closing of our age
  our night becomes as day.
We know our lives are in your hand
  but that we have them back
to live in freedom's light as those
  who belong to eternal day.

2.

Our souls are restless, Lord,
till we find rest in you,
and so, great God our Father,
we turn our thoughts to you.
Refresh us with your grace

and fill our hearts anew,
that we may live for others,
as you would have us do.

3.

O Lord of our tranquility,
    we need your humble care
if we would make the way of peace
    a broadened thoroughfare.
Our heritage is meaningful —
    our lives are without fear —
when we become as one in you
    and keep your presence near.
We walk in shadows fearfully,
    not knowing who we are,
unless your presence lights our way
    as brightly as a star.
Forgive our foolish, head-strong ways,
    that lead to senseless strife,
and wake our hearts to gentleness
    that leads our souls to life,
and gird our souls that they may be
    inclined to liberty,
wherein does lie the cosmic strength
    which makes us truly free.

4.

Your word is life
to all who hear,
and when we call
we find you near —
as near as is
our neighbor's farm,
as near as those
whose lives we harm.
Your word is life
to those who dare
to give their all
without a care —
who seek not self
nor great success,
but just to share
life's happiness.

5.

We hear, O God, your summons here
    to live in harmony,
and so we turn to one another
    and let our love run free.
We cast aside the foolish weights,
    that we have borne so long,
of fear and hate and prejudice
    and raise our hearts in song.
Give ear unto our broken cries
    whenever we hesitate
because of unrepented sins
    that seek to make us wait.
Secure within the love you bring,
    may we our lives begin
as people open to the love
    that conquers every sin.

6.

We see your steadfast love, O God,
    and we are so ashamed
that we have turned away from you
    to seek our wealth and fame.
Our hearts have followed in the steps
    of those whom we despise,
and we are just as guilty, Lord,
    of hatred and of lies.
Forgive us, Lord, for we are all
    ashamed of what we've done
to hinder or prevent your Word
    from making all men one.
Enable us at least to be
    what you would have us be,
and guide us in our daily quest
    to set your people free.

7.

Who walk in shadows never see
the light that makes men free.
Who love refuse to all mankind,
to God are truly blind.
We pray, O Lord, that we may see
the love that sets us free,
and also learn to freely give,

that everyone may live.
Teach us to labor all our days
to lead the world to sing your praise.

8.

We feel your presence near, O Lord;
    it fills our hearts with joy
that nothing in creation can
    inhibit or destroy.
We find ourselves in circumstances
    that try our very soul,
but when we turn to you in prayer
    our lives take on a glow.
The world may storm and rail at us,
    but when we live for you
we find your promises of strength
    to live our lives is true.
To live for you is difficult,
    this no one can deny,
but far more difficult is life
    for those who never try.
Instill your love within us, Lord;
    be with us in this hour,
so that we may avail ourselves
    of your eternal power.

9.

In this brief hour
we cannot find
all the answers
to heart and mind;
but grant, O Lord,
that we may care
for those who in distress
give into deep despair,
and grant that we,
in fellowship today,
may gain the strength
for which we pray.

10.

Divine Redeemer, Lord of life,
send forth your clarion call;
banish the fears and foolish strife

which hold our hearts enthralled.
Open the channels of our minds
to the Holy Spirit's call.

11.

Our God is with us in this hour,
and so we open now our hearts
so that he may come, in all his power,
and cleanse our hearts of wrong desires.
And then we pray he will abide
within our hearts forevermore,
so that from hence we may take pride
in serving him wherever we are.
Come, O Lord, we greet you now;
we promise now to keep our vow.

12.

Condemned to live in loneliness,
your love has led to blessedness,
and so we live in harmony —
no more enslaved but truly free.
We give you thanks for bringing life
where formerly was only strife.
May we, in love, proclaim your name
to all whose lives are lost in shame,
so that they too can come to know
that in your love their lives can grow.

13.

We do not pray for famous tombs
or houses filled with many rooms.
We only pray that we may see
how great is life when truly free.

14.

We walk in shadows, as it were,
    afraid to face the sun,
whenever we refuse to see
    the Christ, your loving Son.
In vain do those pretend to see,
    by selfishness made blind,
who follow lives of senselessness
    with empty, vacant mind.
Be with us, Lord, so we may see

      the loneliness and pain
that call to us to minister
      in Jesus' holy name.
With fervent vow we turn again,
      in answer to your call,
to serve the needy and the blind,
      to dismantle every wall.

15.

We seek you, God, among the joys of life
and when our hearts repose in sorrow's clutch.
In love we speak the truth to one another,
and meet you, Lord, in the lives of those we touch.
We know that when we seek with open eyes,
and with a true concern for what is right,
we find our lives are ever more sustained
by your sweet love, even in our darkest night.

16.

As we behold your face, O Lord,
    we know within our hearts
that all too many times we've failed
    to set a place apart
within our lives to contemplate
    the joy we have in you,
and also to do the many things
    we know you'd have us do.
Content to let the world go by,
    we stay within our shells
while children of our Heavenly King
    walk in a living hell.
Refresh our vision, Lord, we pray,
    so we may come to see
that when we cease to live aloof
    we will be truly free.

17.

Within your love,
we find the way
to brighten up
our darkest day.
We thank you, Lord,
for being here,
for casting out

our every fear.
As we reach out
to lend a hand,
then shall we come
to understand
that blessings come
to those who wait
upon the needy
outside their gate.

18.

We wander from the light,
and often lose our way,
and so with anxious heart
we turn to you today.
Your presence brings us joy
and strengthens us for life,
so come to us, O Lord,
and banish senseless strife.
We give ourselves to you
so our community
may help the world become
a place where all are free.
Your blessings we implore
upon our lives today,
as we join hands to walk
within your holy way.

19.

Our lives become a tidy mess
    when guided by our pride,
and when we meet God on the street
    we pass on the other side.
Our eyes are blinded by our greed,
    unable now to see
the very God who loves us so
    that he has set us free.
He does not claim what is his right
    but trusts instead in love
and seeks to lead us in those ways
    presented by the dove.
We answer, Lord, to your low call
    and give our lives today,
content to let the world go by
    in favor of your way.

20.

God of the wind, the sky, the sea,
you call us to be truly free,
to live our lives in sweet accord,
to be attentive to your Word.
May we begin to live our days
in ways that truly show our praise,
by serving well our native land,
each giving each a helping hand.

21.

Please keep us in your presence, Lord;
remove our fears and vanity.
Take from our hearts our foolish pride
so that our eyes may clearly see
that only as we give ourselves,
and ask for nothing in return,
can we begin to find that peace
for which our hearts so deeply yearn.
We come before you now, O Lord,
content to live within your Word.

22.

Take from our hearts that idleness
which keeps us from your blessedness,
and bless us, Lord, that we may be
your children, ever proud and free.
Help us dare to dream and plan
for ways to make a better land,
so that your love may be the rule,
and man may cease to play the fool.
We give you praise for life and love,
and set our will on things above.

23.

To dream may be an idler's way
    of hiding from the sun,
a way to pass the time of day
    while getting little done.
But busyness can also be
    a way of copping out,
a way of hiding from ourselves
    and every little doubt.
You call us, Lord, to dream your dreams,

    to follow after one
who sought to harness all our powers
    in getting your work done.
Since things are not as they should be,
    we have a need of dreams;
we need to turn ourselves away
    from all our petty schemes.
God send us dreams that we may see
    there is a better way,
and give us courage to embark
    upon that way today.

24.

The Lord, our God, comes close to us
    when we behold his Son,
and we become his instruments
    when we are truly one.
May grace and love abide herein,
    and may our lives become
as holy as our blessed Lord's,
    our Father's noble Son.

25.

We reach unto the Lord,
whence all our lives begin,
and pray that through his love
we may be freed of sin.
His love is all we need
to guide us on our way,
and so we give our hearts
unto the Lord today.
May all men walk in truth
and give their hearts to love
so that the world may know
that God indeed is love.

26.

For freedom you have set us free,
    to live for you alone;
our gaze you've lifted from the ground
    to your almighty throne.
No longer are we satisfied
    with narrowness and greed;
no longer can we look aside

from people in their need;
for you have called us by our name
    and lead us in the way
that brings a new tomorrow near
    and brightens up today.

27.

Have mercy on us, Lord,
when we refuse to see
the very subtle bonds
that keep the poor unfree.
At times we're slow to learn
the lessons you would teach
and cannot see the needs
just out beyond our reach.
Our grasp is oh so small,
our vision oh so weak,
that we can seldom hear
the message that you speak.
Help us to be aware
of what your children need
so that, from selfish greed,
our lives at last are freed.

28.

Your presence, Lord,
so frees our hearts,
for to our lives
your love imparts
a joyful glow
of blessedness,
and then we know
your gentleness.
Implant in us
your love divine
so that our lives,
like fruitful vines,
may bring your word
to all humankind,
life to the dying,
sight to the blind.

29.

O Lord, be present in our lives,
    wherever we may be;

uphold us by your righteous laws
    in perfect liberty.
Oh teach us by your loving grace
    to value who we are,
and teach us by your judgments clear
    to value every star.
We need your love to stand alone
    against a godless world,
and, Lord, we need your guiding hand
    to make a better world.
Forgive our lack of self-control,
    and guide us in your way,
so that our lives may be a star
    to show the brighter way.

30.

Our lives are sacred in your sight,
    as life can plainly show
to those who have the faith and love
    within your way to go.
Please make us instruments of peace
    to those now lost in fear,
and let our lives confirm to them
    that you are truly here.

31.

In silence and in solitude
    we contemplate your way
of leading us to righteousness
    when we take time to pray.
We often fail to stop and think,
    before we start our day,
of where we really want to go,
    and so we go astray.
Open our eyes that we may see,
    our hearts that we may know,
so that, within your blessed grace,
    our lives may ever grow.
Teach us to be aware of love
    and what it means to be
a people ever consecrated
    to setting others free.

32.

We delight in the Lord,
in the light of his Word,
for he has spoken love
to those who hear his Word.
Our shame we cannot hide
for we have chosen death —
but still in him abide
our lives and all we are.
He will not let us go,
but reaches out his hand
in loving tenderness
we dimly understand.
Oh call us to your side
and cast away our fears,
for we will ever abide
in love that knows no peer.

33.

We pray your presence, Lord,
will here abide —
that we may hear your call
and cease to deny.
Open up our eyes and ears,
that we may see and hear,
and thus may know, without a doubt,
the time for serving you is here.

34.

Behold us, Lord,
as here we stand;
we give our hearts
into your hand.
We promise here
to do our best
to spread your Word,
and never rest
until your love
has conquered all,
and bridges tower
over every wall.

35.

When we can give ourselves to you,

with lives set free from sin
and uncorrupted by the world,
    true love can enter in.
Your love can fill our hearts with joy
    whenever we are true
to all the tasks you give to us
    upon this earth to do.
And so we tune our hearts to you
    and let our souls run free,
so that our lives once more may be,
    by love, set truly free.

36.

Come, Lord, deliver us, we pray —
create in us a joyful heart
that we might learn to live today,
not waiting till tomorrow comes
to live the life that we should lead.
Forgive us for our foolishness,
that blinds our hearts to those in need,
and leads us to your blessedness,
that opens up our hearts and lives
so that we live and love indeed.

37.

There is a gentleness to love,
    so hard to imitate,
that those who seek to play a game
    are wise to hesitate
before they show their grace-less state
    to all with eyes to see.
But first to God let us repair,
    whose love can set us free,
and then, in truth, we can extend
    ourselves in loving care;
and those we meet upon the street
    will know we truly care;
for sharing is the name of love,
    and those who truly yearn
to let their love be genuine
    this truth must truly learn:
When we can give without a thought
    of what our gain may be,
then we will find, for God and man,
    our love has set us free.

38.
Forgive our selfish thoughts, O Lord,
and lead us in the way
that we should go, and teach us now
the words that we should say,
and help us purify our hearts and lives
by living love each day.

39.

We have no fear
for God is here —
his presence fills our hearts.
He speaks with love
and sends the dove
of peace to anguished hearts.
The anguished soul
forgets all woe
when wrapped within his love,
for fear departs
when human hearts
are opened to his love.

40.

Each gift is bare,
of little worth,
if love's not there;
and so, O Lord,
we do intend
to give ourselves
until we mend
this strife-torn world.
Be with us now,
and grant that we
may keep our vow
to set men free
from hate and fear;
give us the love
to perservere
in our intent.

41.

We live —
for life is ours!
We do not fear

the darkest powers,
because we see
the blessed light
that shines within
the darkest night.
That light divine
we now perceive
abides with those
who dare believe
that justice reigns,
though cruel night
for now may fill
our hearts with fright.
Today your love
can fill our heart,
if with your love
we play our part.

42.

We open up our hearts, O Lord,
    and seek your presence here,
because we know your perfect love
    can vanquish all our fear.
Within our homes we give you place,
    and all our lives we give
to seek those souls, now lost in sin,
    who know not how to live.
Our cross we gladly bear, O Lord,
    nor will we turn aside
till all humankind your presence feels
    and in your love abides.

43.

The Lord is here:
as near as our neighbor
who stands in need;
as near as the sun
which warms our bodies;
as near as the water
which quenches our thirst;
as near as the love
which stirs our souls.
Blessed be God
and all his children,

and may we live in love
as he would have us do.

44.

The cross-cursed Christ calls ceaselessly,
but fear stops our ears.
Crisis follows crisis with no release,
but arrogance dulls our senses.
Speak loud and clear, Lord,
so that your voice may pierce
the dullness of our hearing,
so that your love may penetrate
to the depths of our hearts.
Then will we know your peace;
then will we be children of the loving God.

45.

Please keep us in your presence, Lord:
remove our fears and vanity.
Take from our hearts our foolish pride
so that our eyes may clearly see
that only as we give ourselves,
and ask for nothing in return,
can we begin to find that peace
for which our hearts so deeply yearn.
We come before you now, O Lord,
content to live within your Word.

46.

We pray for peace where there is war,
    for love where hate now reigns.
We pray that joy may follow sorrow
    as flowers follow rain.
May we be freed of everything
    that blinds us to your call,
and softly may your words of love
    upon our senses fall.
Eternal is your love, O Lord,
    and justice is your way,
and we are called to live our lives
    as children of the day.
We give ourselves in penance now
    for all that we have done,
and promise not to turn aside

till all the world is one.
As we begin to live our lives,
    in ways where Christ has led,
we pledge ourselves to free the blind,
    whose spirits now are dead.

47.

Forgive, O Lord, our foolish fears,
    that blind us to your love,
and help us turn our down-cast eyes
    unto the heights above.
We seek in haste for passing things,
    which quickly disappear;
just when we think the battle's won
    new challenges appear.
May we, in faith, turn unto you,
    the true and living Word,
content to leave pursuit of power
    to those who know no Lord.
Our lives are yours, for you alone
    have power to set us free,
and now, O Lord, we look to you
    with eyes that truly see.
We only ask of you one thing:
To teach our hearts with love to sing!

48.

The victory is ours,
for we have found the Lord
in whom our God and King
has shown his holy Word.
May we and all humankind
within his love abide,
so that these wars of hate
may one day all subside.
Then we may learn to live
in true community,
where everyone holds dear
for each his liberty.
Come to us now, O Lord,
so we at last may be
from all our foolish pride
eternally set free.

49.

Come, Lord,
hear our grateful prayers;
send us where you need
our loving care.
We trust in you and pray
that, through your guidance,
we will come to know of love
that never stops
to count the cost.

50.

Let our world
have your blessing, God.
Remain with us
no matter what may happen.
Give us from your hand
our lives, with all
its cares and pleasures.
Teach us that life
which Christ came to show
to all who have eyes to see.

51.

We are yours, O God,
and gladness fills our hearts
to know that you chose us
to play a mighty part
within your plan for us.
Teach us, Lord, to seek
your living presence here
in everything we do,
letting neither peace nor fear
destroy our love for you.

52.

We see you in the glory
of ages that are gone,
and in the eager brightness
of early morning dawn.
Though clouds be dark around us,
we follow now your light,
not caring what the multitude
may choose to call the right.

No words can ever sway us
   from following the way
that Christ has shown will bring us
   into a brighter day.

53.

We heed, O Lord, your call to come
   and seek you in this place.
We gladly hear your clarion call
   which nothing can erase.
We lay our lives upon your altar,
   not asking for the light
we need to see our way but trusting
   that you will lead us right.
Shed forth your light within our hearts
   so we may see within
and know ourselves for what we are,
   and what we might have been.
Help us to follow in the way
   that leads to truth and light,
content to work for nothing less
   than what we believe is right.

54.

Our Lord is come! Our hearts are gay,
for life is fresh and new each day.
God does not hide his face from us,
and so we know that we can trust.
We can believe what we have heard,
for God reveals the living Word.
When we forget our silly rules,
we cease to be such silly fools.
The Word is found when we are free
to let men love and let men be.

55.

We hear the Lord in quietness
and when our lives his love confess.
This noisy world, with all its lust,
can undermine our greatest trust.
Be with us, God; incline our ears
to hear your Word as we draw near.

56.

Teach us to be open, Lord,
to life and love and you,
so that our lives may be as fresh
as early morning dew.
Ease the pain within our hearts
and grant that peace of mind
which comes from resting in your love
and serving all mankind.
Grant that we may ever find
that deep tranquility
where love and joy and peace abide
in true community.
Teach each one to bless your name
with deep humility
that vaunts not self but rests content
within humanity.

57.

We come before your presence, Lord,
    intent on finding life,
for we have lived too long, it seems,
    with empty, selfish strife.
Forgive our sinful self-regard,
    that knows no sacrifice,
and fill our hearts with your sweet love,
    which conquers every vice.
Come guide us in your gentle way,
    so void of thoughts of harm,
so we may end hostilities
    with gentle, loving arms.
May we, in love, reach out to those
    whom we can scarcely abide
and give our lives in thoughtful zeal,
    with no attempt to hide.

58.

Come to us, O Lord;
inspire our hearts with joy.
Teach us in every day
our gifts of life to employ
in never-ending praise
of your great glory here.
Open our hearts to love

and banish all our fear,
so that our lives may be
a song of celebration,
and not an empty act
of vainglorious oblation.

59.

Lead us, Lord, when we are blind.
Forgive us when we are unkind.
Emerge in us and show the way;
guide us in our work and play.
Time, unmeasured, clouds our view,
and, even though our hearts are true,
we find it difficult to see
a path that leads us through the debris
of lives unfocused and apart.
Help us this day to make a start
towards being what we can be
by learning to be completely free.

60.

The Lord before us stands
with blood upon his hands.
What will our answer be
to him who set us free?
Will we his love confess
and give to him our best?
Or will we turn away
and say, "Some other day"?
We know, despite our fear,
that you are ever near,
and so with all our hearts
we swear to do our part
to spread your blessed love
to those who know no love.
Be with us as we strive
to make this world alive.

61.

Eternal God, we here confess
our lack of love, the shallowness
that keeps us from your divine love.
Our lives are like the fruit-less vine.
Forgive us, Lord, and help us know

the life of hearts with love aglow.
Enter our hearts and help us be
your heirs indeed — at last born free!

62.

Your presence fills our hearts, O Lord,
    when we receive your grace,
and yet we often turn our backs,
    afraid to see your face.
We fear responsibility,
    and all that it entails
of selflessness and brotherhood
    and seeing without veils.
Please soothe away our many fears,
    and teach us tenderness
so that our lives may intertwine
    and each the other bless.

63.

So many people walk in chains
    that they don't even see;
so many now are so enslaved
    when they most think they're free.
True freedom is a precious thing,
    and yet so quickly lost
when we so glibly speak as if
    it came without a cost.
But worst of all the things to see
    are those so truly blind
who in the very name of freedom
    would fetter all men's minds.

Poetry

1. Ghosts of Days Gone By

Beware of theologians bold,
    by minor passions bit,
who turn their haughty warrior's gaze
    against the tiny nit,
while camels swiftly slip that grasp,
    too small to do them harm,
which now contentedly surveys
    its own irresistable charm.
I'd laugh, if it were not so sad,
    at passionate defense
of creeds and airy castle walls
    and noble battlements,
which long held firm against fiery trials
    and enemies so bold,
who long since fled the battlefield,
    while they've grown cold and old.
But battles fought and victories won
    will take from us a toll,
and walls thus firmly laid and bound
    can lose their very soul.
With eyes glazed, their weary glance
    now sees as through a haze;
not knowing that their foes have fled,
    they fight with senseless craze.

they fight with senseless craze.
They fight with such a noble mein
    a losing, winning fight,
and strive so hard to bring to pass
    a well established "Right."
The world addresses them direct,
    with earnest, anxious pleas,
for help against their deadly foes,
    whom our friends can't even see.
And on they fight their noble fight,
    not ever asking why,
so blinded to the light of day,
    and deaf when real needs cry,
that enemies so bold and strong
    can glide so swiftly by,
while they are locked in battlements
    against ghosts of days gone by.

2. Ode to a Blithe Spirit

You've gone upstairs,
it's plain to see,
cause Satan'd never stand
such levity.
Your blitheful spirit
would weigh him down
until he chased
you out of town.
And so with God
you'd have to be —
I'm sure he'd love
your levity.
You're kindred spirits,
you and he —
in life and love
you're truly free.

3. An Endless Quest?

The agonizing Job,
with children dead
and cattle gone,
the crying child,
whose pet
the speeding car destroys,
are kindred souls.

What pain to lose a friend,
to watch as doves and hawks
destroy the world we love.
What sense may we espy
where senseless hate
destroys its own?
Fools may quickly claim
to see a purpose here,
but agony within
cannot be stilled by aspirin.

4. Bells Are for Ringing

I cannot mourn for very long,
for life was meant to be a song,
and, though dirges must be sung,
the bells, too, must be rung.
Our hearts were meant to be the string
on which the love of God can sing
the praise of all that he has made.
And though a heavy weight be laid
upon my heart, I must depart
from useless thoughts and take the part,
once more, which I've been called to play
in hastening a brighter day.
I can't be sad too long, it seems,
for God continues placing dreams
within my heart, and though some fail,
and to my life bring great travail,
I'll still proclaim the Father's love
is to be treasured far above
the petty pace of daily life
devoid of every little strife,
for such a life bears too much cost
and is the lot of those who've lost
the sight of God's so great design
that's meant to bring a world in line
with all that's good, gentle, and kind.
Take up your life, and you will find
that darkness cannot long abide
within a heart that will not hide.

5. Pursuing a Nameless Star

In silent wonder
I pursue a star

that glows
but dimly.
What lures me on
through friendless days
in vain pursuit
of broken dreams?
At times I plod,
and then I fly,
sustained
by unknown springs.
I cannot quit
but know not why.
Unwilling flesh,
and fainting spirit,
go on,
forever asking, "Why?"

6. Here I Stand

Here I stand,
doubting Thomas though I am.
Though the winds of hell may pound me,
still the love of God surrounds me.
Never was a promise made
I would not ever be dismayed.
So from my lips no plaintiff cry,
even should I have to die.
Let others have their certainty,
I will live on charity.
All I ask, along the way,
is light sufficient for the day.

7. It's Easy to Sing

It's easy to sing when the wind fills your sail,
but when rains come down faster than pails can bail,
    we discover what we are made of.
It's easy to smile when skies are fair,
but when storms start to strip our souls till they're bare,
    only then do we know our love.
For love that is shallow will hide from the pain,
and smiles that are empty, will fade with the rain,
    and hearts that are faint will be done.
If love is for real, our suffering will reveal
a soul that can swim with the ease of an eel,
    and our life will have only begun.

8. None Ere Shall Say

Although the cause may fail for which I strive,
I'll not, by failure's fear, be turned aside
from following that which makes my heart alive,
nor from the barbs of fools my conscience hide.
The world may ever with oblations serve
some cause which great renown or profits brings;
I give my heart to God without reserve
and set my mind and heart on heavenly things.
It may well be that I shall not succeed —
at least I'll never sell my soul for naught.
Whatever the end of all my life may be,
no one shall every say I have not fought.
Let life bring to me what it will of pain;
I'll know my life has not been lived in vain.

9. A Higher Call

Intrepid men, by minor passions bent,
desert their souls and seek a sad surcease
from pain, not knowing that time is only lent,
and that their foolish labors just increase
the woe they seek to end; the more we spend
our time on little things that seldom count
within the scheme of things; the more we bend
our ways to little men; the less we'll amount
to when the scales are weighed. It never pays
to sacrifice our song for a minor tune;
though people here may loudly sing our praise,
we are, in truth, no better than a loon.
We must be true to a higher call if we
desire to be at peace and "truly free."

10. The Piety of Doubt

With softly folded hands we wait
before the awesome throne of fate.
Before our souls are very old,
we learn to do as we are told.
The pious phrasing that we hear
so quickly comes to be so dear
that God himself must stand aside
and let us take our lives in stride —
in stride with what we do not know,
but since our words from parents flow,
we dare not stop to question why —

for unbelievers surely die!
And thus their words we will repeat —
sentimental, soft, and sweet.
Disquietude we never know —
impiety we never show.
Doubt is as far beyond our sod —
as is the everlasting God.

11. The Torch of Truth

What good is love when it is blind?
Sightless eyes will never find
the path God meant for them to take,
and empty brains will quickly break
the bonds that love was meant to forge.
God gives to us a burning torch
to show our twisted path. We hide
the torch within a tub and guide
our steps by precepts tried and true,
and when our way is filled with undue
hardship, we fail to see the part
our foolishness has played. We start
and stop, not knowing where to go.
The torch of truth alone can show
the path to us, so let us cease
from folly. In wisdom lies our peace.

12. Dreams and Nightmares

A beautiful memory
of yesteryear,
faded photographs;
tender memories
rendered mute,
timeless,
beautiful to behold.
Yet lovely dreams
nourish nightmares,
deadly in their dullness —
so subtle
we think ourselves alive
amid the decay
of memorabilia.

13. Afraid to See

We sit and wait,

and hope that fate
will bring us peace.
Yet nothing comes
to those who wait.
But empty years
will never show
the error of our ways.
Afraid to see,
we tell ourselves a tale —
and yet the need
we feel inside
convinces us that what we hide
just really can't be true.
And so we wait —
and God, and life, and love
remain a dream.

14. The Journey of Death

Death is a journey,
not an end, one more trip
to visit a friend.
Each step of the way
someone has gone before,
and friends are there
to greet us at the door.
I do not fear
this trip I take,
for I am sure
I will awake
to greet my friends,
and also find
the one whose life
bought peace of mind.

15. The Bitter Choice (on a friend's suicide)

Each one must choose if length of days
is something worthy of our praise,
    if life alone is worth the cost
    when all our joy in life is lost,
and nothing pleasing meets our gaze.
No one can choose for us the ways
we seek to lead us through the maze
    of storm-filled seas that must be crossed.
        Each one must choose!

So do not curse the one who lays
aside his life as if a craze
    for dying filled his soul. Those tossed
    aside by life must soon accost
that fate we see as through a haze.
      Each one must choose!

16. Death Is a River

Death is a river flowing by,
with shady lane and friends close by,
a blest relief from summer sun
when our life's work is over and done.
So do not mourn this trip I take,
and do not give a mournful wake,
for I had finished what I started
before my soul this life departed.
I do not leave one task behind
whose lack of finish I should mind.
 I lived a life that was complete,
so tales of woe please don't repeat.
Instead, remember what I'd done
before my final rest was won,
and thank the Lord for what has been
and for the prizes you may win,
if you will live your life as though
    death were your friend and not your foe.

17. Simple Words and Ways

Some praise the Lord with loud "Amen!"
and pour forth thanks
with empty words and vain oblations
that do not touch their stone-cold hearts.
Yet others think
that by their words they please the God
of this great universe,
and so they choose, with tender care,
their great long words,
and seek by pomp and circumstance
to dazzle ears
unused to such a sweet array
of empty sounds.
And sad to say,
such words impress so greatly
that the people, thus deluded,

cry for more.
But simple words serve better still
to show our praise,
and best of all
are thankful hearts
that turn our lives around
until, without a glance,
We turn aside from busy ways
to give a cup to those who thirst,
and feed the poor,
not for some rich reward we hope to earn,
but just because the need is there.
All other praise is vain indeed
when we fulfill each other's need.

18. Reaching Out

Dry bones that bleach in the desert sun
breed fear and hate in everyone,
and make us prone to hide away,
afraid to face the coming day.
Callousness becomes the rule,
and law becomes a deadly tool,
where we pretend a higher law,
yet live by bloody tooth and claw.
Disdainfully we judge the poor,
and turn the beggar from our door;
desperate men find no relief
before our awesome judgment seat.
Foolishly, we will not see
how senseless is our rivalry,
how we destroy the peace we seek
by turning from the poor and weak.
Give! and in the giving find
love alone brings peace of mind.

19. We Are our Jailer

We are our jailer.
We are the one
who closes the door
to shut out the sun.
No one can close it
without our consent,
so, when freedom is gone,
we know where it went.

The coward will earn
his own just reward —
a two-by-four cell
without any door.
Although his own victim,
he'll rant and he'll rave
against the despoilers
who "fashioned" his cave.
Desire to be free
is never enough.
True freedom's pain
calls for sterner stuff.
We are our jailer.
We are the one
to open the door —
if ever it's done.

20. The Judging Place

It's easier by far, it seems,
to face our end when we have dreams,
when we have lived as Christ decreed,
as friend to those in dire need.
If we, by fear, are turned aside,
or hide behind our silly pride,
then Christ himself will hide his face
when we approach the judging place.
And yet, though warned of our sad fate,
we turn aside and deprecate
the very ones who need our prayers,
And then we dare to put on airs,
as if we lived beyond reproach.
Our lives would shame the lowly roach,
who lives at least as God intends,
while foolish man so soon offends
the God to whom he turns in prayer.
God only comes to those who dare
to put aside all thoughts of rage,
who won't bow down to this cruel age.
 For Christ proclaimed a jubilee,
a time for people to be free,
a time when love should rule the day,
when thoughts of revenge are put away.

21. Freedom or Tyranny?

My heart cries out —
the pain subsides,
but still I cry, though silently.
The ache within is measureless,
and hides behind serenity
more false than real.
I cry for you,
for me, for them,
for all who facetiously —
as if our past were not destroyed,
our future dark and perilous.
We will not see —
we blind our eyes with vain pretense.
We pipe and dance and sing a song,
content to go along with faceless crowds.
We will not hear —
though death's dark cry rings soundlessly
in halls bereft of liberty,
where all have fled
and seek release in tyranny.
We pay its cost more readily,
for freedom's sway demands far more
than paltry prayers
for selfish ends.
But when at last the balance falls,
and we are left with nothing —
then shall our eyes,
too late, be clear
as we survey all we hold dear
destroyed by fire —
by fire that we ourselves create
when we deny to anyone
the justice we pervert so soon
to our own ends.

22. When Trials Are Promises

The peace of God be with you now,
    with each and every one,
so that your lives may know the joy
    of Christmas truly come.
And may the wilderness of life,
    and the desert of your way,
become transformed by the Christ Event

upon this Christmas Day.
Our gracious God has given us
    a reason to rejoice,
so let us all respond today
    with heart and hand and voice.
Of what was once a wilderness
    there is no more a trace,
and we can now rejoice within
    our solitary place.
Learn from the rose its secret now,
    whereby, with loving care,
a beautiful and fragrant flower
    lends fragrance to the air.
It does take toil, and constant care,
    to grow the wondrous rose,
and it takes toil to form a life
    that still more godly grows,
but the reward is worth the toil,
    and also worth the pain,
for God has given us the promise
    of everlasting gain.
Our trials, then, are promises
    of joy we yet will see,
and suffering in the name of God
    will teach us to be free.